Authority in Morals

Authority in Morals

An Essay in Christian Ethics

Gerard J. Hughes

GEORGETOWN UNIVERSITY PRESS

Library of Congress Cataloging in Publication Data
Hughes, Gerard J.
   Authority in morals.
   Reprint. Originally published/ London: Heythrop
College, 1978. (Heythrop monographs, ISSN 0309-4723; 3)
   Bibliography: p.
   1. Christian ethics—Catholic authors. 2. Authority—
Moral and ethics aspects.   I. Title.
BJ1249.H78   1984   241   84-4009
ISBN 0-87840-410-4

CONTENTS

TO MY PARENTS

With gratitude for their teaching
and their example

ACKNOWLEDGEMENTS

I would like to thank above all my Jesuit colleagues Frs John Mahoney and John Russell, and also Fr Kevin Kelly of the Up Holland Northern Institute, who read earlier versions of this essay, and made many helpful criticisms. I would also like to thank Mrs Janice Thomas for her criticisms of Chapters II and III. Needless to say, they should not be taken as subscribing to everything which I have written, but I have found the effort of meeting their criticisms extremely helpful. I would also gratefully acknowledge the permission given by the editors of *The Heythrop Journal* and *Theological Studies* to use, in Chapters I and IV, material which appeared in an earlier version in the pages of their journals.

Introduction

This is a book about method in moral theology, written in the conviction that the present state of the subject in the Christian community at large as well as in the Roman Catholic Church to which I belong is bedevilled by a lack of any clear understanding of how Christians ought to approach moral problems. This is also a book about authority, because it seems to me that the central issue of method which divides moral theologians concerns the role which authorities of various kinds should play in their arguments. On some views, the final and even the only source from which the Christian should derive his morality is to be found in the Bible (or, at any rate, in the New Testament). Others would maintain that later Christian tradition as it is embodied in the teachings of Popes, Councils, and the moral theologians of the Church is either an essential supplement to the biblical teaching, or is essential in order to maintain an authentic understanding of that teaching. Others might argue that it is the consensus of all Christian believers which should ultimately determine the moral beliefs of the Christian community. Others, finally, might hold that the only authority in morals is the authority of one's own conscience, where a man finally stands alone before God.

Differences of opinion about the role of these alleged authorities lead inevitably to differences of method in moral theology. To the extent that some text, be it the Bible or the writings of Councils or Popes, is taken to be the ultimate moral authority, the proper method to be followed will consist in endeavouring to discover what authority has said, and in making sure that it is properly understood and interpreted. Moral conclusions and beliefs will be justified just in so far as they can be shown to be derived from the teaching of the competent authority. On the other hand, a moral theology which lays stress on the authority of the *sensus fidelium* will presumably pay less attention to the Bible or to papal encyclicals, and will presumably also have to elaborate some method of discovering just what kind of agreement is to be taken as the authentic consensus of the believing community. Again, if the authority of conscience is contrasted with all these other authorities, the entire role and approach of moral theology will be viewed quite differently.

It will be convenient here to offer some preliminary remarks on why I am assuming throughout what follows that there is a need of some defensible method in moral theology, and to give an initial outline of the arguments I shall put forward in favour of the method I propose.

My assumption that there is a need for *some* method in morals or in moral theology might be attached at its very roots by the flat assertion that the whole notion of method is out of place in ethics, and that all that is required is that a person should act according to his conscience. Equally flatly, it might be replied that method is essential. More constructively, I think that the need for method can be established only by showing the utility of adopting some particular method, and this I shall try to do in stages; in Chapter II I shall try to show how adopting a particular method will help towards the development of personal moral knowledge; in Chapter III, I shall argue that this method will throw light on our attitude to and use of moral principles; and in the last two chapters I shall try to present a picture of the way in which this method might find expression in the life of the Christian community. I do not believe that there is any possibility of a logical proof to demonstrate that any method ought to be followed. The most that can be done is to show that some problems in which we are interested are insoluble, so far as we can see, unless a particular method is adopted. If someone is not interested in those problems, or fails to see the attractiveness of the proposed solutions, logic will certainly not help.

On the other hand, it will help to clear away some possible mis-conceptions, such as that to propose the adoption of method in ethics is somehow to undermine the ultimate dignity of the indivi-dual conscience. More will be said on this topic later. For the moment, I would like to make it clear that it is important to insist that a person should follow his conscience. The alternative would seem to be that instead of making conscientious decisions we should simply act on impulse, or unthinkingly go along with the crowd, or accept the views of others. But although it is important to say that a person ought to follow his conscience, it is also a truism; it is to say no more than that a person ought to act as he believes it to be his duty to act. So far, we have been told nothing about how such beliefs might be supported, challenged, or estab-lished. To say that I must abide by my conscientious decision is to give me no assistance at all in knowing how such a decision is to be arrived at. To do that, something must be said about the *method* of ethics.

It will be evident from my use of such expressions as 'belief', 'support' and 'establish' that I am assuming a cognitivist position in ethics. That is to say, I believe that moral utterances can be true or false, and that it is perfectly legitimate to speak of moral views as being mistaken, well-founded, or ill-supported, and of moral arguments as being valid, invalid, or inadequate, just as it is in other areas of rational discourse. Only by adopting a basically cognitivist position, it seems to me, is it possible to do justice to such ordinary features of our moral lives as wondering what we really ought to do, or whether our decision was after all a mistaken one, or to such notions as moral perceptiveness or sensitivity. Non-cognitivist accounts of the former in terms of being unable to decide what we shall do and wondering whether we are willing to live by our decision once taken, seem to me unconvincing as accounts of what we normally take to be going on in such situations. And even non-cognitivists like Hare are willing to allow that ordinary usage should be decisive in such matters. I do not wish to give a full-scale criticism of non-cognitivist ethics here. Suffice it to say that in adopting a cognitivist position I have committed myself to the view that the notions of truth and mistake are as important in ethics as they are in any other area of human knowledge, and therefore I need to discover some method for discovering where the truth in ethics lies.

In so saying, I am not assuming that I necessarily will discover the correct method to use in arriving at moral decisions, nor that, even if I do discover it, I will infallibly succeed in using it aright in any particular case. On the contrary, I suppose that the method I shall be proposing is unlikely to prove fully adequate, despite my best efforts to make it so; and I imagine, too, that all of us make mistakes in our moral decisions. I would insist, however, that to say that one cannot always be blamed for making mistakes, or that one has a duty to act as one believes to be right, even when (as it happens) one is mistaken in this belief, is quite different from saying that no mistake has been made. I may well end up by doing the wrong thing, in one sense, even if in another sense it was the right thing for me to do, and I may well be in a position to say of someone else that what he did was wrong, even when I would not blame him (and might even wish to praise him) for having done it.

For these reasons, then, I am interested in problems of method in ethics, and I believe that to insist on the importance of method in ethics is not in any way to undermine the dignity of the individual conscience nor to advocate moral intolerance.

Because this is a book about method, the burning problems of the day will find a place in these pages only occasionally and as illustrations offered in passing. To try to deal with such problems directly would, in my view, be quite fruitless in default of any agreed method by which they are to be approached. Anyone who found the conclusions reached about some particular problem unpalatable is likely to reject them simply by saying that the method by which they were arrived at is indefensible — the right authorities were not consulted, or not understood; the wrong kind of arguments were invoked, or the evidence adduced was inadequate or misleading. Moral theology has in recent years had more than enough of *this* kind of debate. Instead, I shall try to highlight the difficulties about method which, as it seems to me, underlie the controversies which rage on particular issues in ethics.

I have already stated one assumption on which my whole approach to ethics is based, in saying that I am an unrepentant cognitivist in ethics. I should also make a second assumption clear, that problems of method are ultimately philosophical problems. I believe that this holds true even in theology, and even in moral theology. I do not, of course, mean that theology is simply a branch of philosophy, any more than physics is. Nor do I mean that philosophers somehow predetermine the conclusions which theologians ought to reach, any more than that philosophers of science predetermine the conclusions to be reached by scientific research. But I do mean that, just as it is legitimate for philosophers to discuss the meaning, status, and legitimacy of conclusions in physics, so it is equally their business to discuss the meaning, status, and legitimacy of the conclusions of theologians. I regard this book as an attempt to show that philosophy, and especially moral philosophy, has a great deal to offer moral theology. It is my conviction that moral theology (with some honourable recent exceptions) has become increasingly out of touch with contemporary moral philosophy, very much to its own detriment. I was once very struck when an eminent American moral philosopher asked me why it was that moral theologians, even those whom he would on general grounds have expected to show more respect for philosophy, wrote in a way which he would never have accepted from an undergraduate student in moral philosophy. He went on to cite some well-known contemporary examples, rich mines of fallacious arguments and unexamined assumptions. I was ashamed at having no ready defence to offer. I regard this book as an attempt to go some way towards meeting that criticism.

The basic problems of method in moral theology, as I believe, concern the ways in which appeal is made to authorities of different kinds. The strategy of the argument I shall present is based on this belief. An initial outline may be helpful at this point.

The most obvious court of appeal in moral theology is the teaching of Christian moral tradition, as this finds expression either in the Bible or in later documents of that tradition. In harmony with this approach is the view that there is a specifically Christian ethic, which it is the task of moral theology to expound by reflection on the data of the specifically Christian revelation. In so far as this revelation is taken to be authoritative in ethics, it is taken to be in some sense an ultimate, which is not open to further criticism from sources external to itself. Against this view, I propose two basic types of difficulty. The first is theological in character. I argue that the picture of God which inevitably emerges from this kind of approach is one which Christians are themselves unwilling to accept consistently. On this model, I argue, God must emerge as an arbitrary figure who would have no legitimate claim on our belief or our allegiance; yet one of the clearest themes of the Judaeo-Christian tradition in the Bible is that God is someone whom man can accept as the ultimate answer to his legitimate aspirations. Any theory of revelation which denies this must in the end leave revelation itself deprived of its credentials. In particular, God must be seen as morally acceptable if we are to have any reason for believing that it is indeed God who is speaking to us. Secondly, I propose some more philosophical objections to this position. It is characteristic of the Christian religion that God reveals himself in history, and therefore in a particular culture at a particular time and place. The texts of Christian tradition in which that revelation is communicated to us are, by the same token, texts of a particular human community at different periods of its development. As such, these texts raise all the philosophical problems of interpretation and translation raised by any text. It follows that the meaning of these texts cannot simply be read off automatically from the texts themselves. In order to establish their meaning we have to have recourse to other assumptions and arguments which the texts themselves do not provide. Moreover, there is an underlying similarity between the problems of translating texts into another language, understanding them within the terms of a different cultural environment, and applying their teaching to different situations. These problems, too, cannot be solved except by appeal to other more primitive assumptions which the texts themselves can do nothing to justify. On both counts, then, it cannot be the case that the texts of Christian tradition are ultimate in any moral argument. Prior assumptions must be made in order to understand them; and some of these prior assumptions must be moral in character. This argument will apply to the Bible; but it will apply in just the same way to any other texts of subsequent Christian tradition, none of which can therefore be taken as ultimately authoritative for Christian ethics.

The second chapter endeavours to be more positive in character by examining and defending some alternative basic assumptions in morals which do not themselves depend on revelation, and can effectively be used in order to interpret and apply the teaching of Christian revelation to ethics. In this chapter, I set out to examine what a moral theory should in principle be like. To begin with, I discuss briefly the difference between a moral theory and other types of theory, firstly in terms of their subject matter, and then in terms of their data and the type of explanation they provide of that data. This in turn leads to a discussion of the characteristics of the basic assumptions which can find a place in an acceptable moral theory. I hope to show that an acceptable moral theory must be in terms of particular human needs. A theory of this type can be considered as a modern version of a natural law theory, at least in its spirit and approach if not in its conclusions. In particular, it will be open to the objections urged against all theories of this type, that they will either be uncritically accepting towards no matter what human needs, real or alleged; or else, they will be viciously circular in the way in which the 'less desirable' needs are excluded. Much of the chapter will be devoted to an effort to show that it is possible to give an account of authentic human needs which is both acceptable and not viciously circular. The conclusion of this inquiry will be that arguments about moral values will depend on factual evidence which is not itself directly moral in character. It is to this factual evidence that appeal in any moral argument will ultimately be made. The ultimate authority in ethics is, in this sense, the authority of non-moral facts, and method in ethics must be based on this truth.

In the third chapter, two kinds of problem are considered concerning the way in which authority is attributed to moral principles in ethical argument. The first problem is whether in some sense moral principles might be properly taken to express some duties which are absolute, in such a way that appeal to such principles can be made in order to settle individual problems without more ado. A distinction is drawn between the assertion that a type of action is intrinsically obligatory and the assertion that it is absolutely obligatory. It is then argued that it is not theoretically possible to have moral principles which express absolute obligations in such a way that these principles can be used to settle particular cases without further moral discussion. The second type of problem concerns the relationship between a true moral principle and the moral agent. To what extent is it true that the moral principle has some kind of external authority over the individual agent and his conscience? It is argued that a great deal of misunderstanding has been caused by the misleading assimilation of moral principles to laws and to commands or imperatives. In harmony with the cognitivist stand of the argument as a whole, it is held that moral principles can have precisely that authority which any other true assertions have. On the other hand, there is more to be said about the connection between moral truths and motivation, as a result of which we can better understand why it is that holding a moral belief does not always feel like holding a belief about some more emotively neutral topic. To this extent, the emotivist contention that the force of evaluative utterances is distinct from the force of purely descriptive utterances seems to be perfectly correct. In this context, too, we can understand why it is that moral principles, and any theory which upholds their importance, can come to be viewed as unwanted and unwarranted intrusions upon the liberty of the individual conscience.

In the light of this discussion, it is now possible to reassess the claims to authoritativeness which have been advanced on behalf of Christian tradition in a more positive light than that in which they were viewed in the first chapter. Chapter IV accordingly begins with an analysis of the circumstances in which it is legitimate to appeal to authority. Obviously, the appeal cannot be ultimate, since, as was argued in Chapter II, the ultimate authority in ethics is the authority of the facts. Nevertheless, there is a legitimate appeal to the authority of Christian tradition, the validity of which is enhanced when the nature of its authority is not misunderstood or overstated. Though the source of the authoritativeness of Christian tradition is different, the logic of the argument in which it is appealed to is no different from the logic of the argument in appealing to authority in any other area of human knowledge.

This remains true even in the special case of the Catholic belief in the possibility of infallible teaching authority in moral matters. The notion of infallibility is analysed in such a way as to distinguish it clearly from the view that infallible truths are timeless truths. The discussion then uses the results of Chapter III on moral principles, so that it becomes clear what can and cannot be expected of an infallible teaching authority in morals.

It emerges from this that the appeal to the authority of Christian tradition will not suffice to solve all the problems of a natural law theory in ethics. In particular, it will not enable us to justify the belief that there is just one defensible solution to all moral problems. It might seem as if the result of the inquiry is in effect a relativist position. However, I argue that the precise nature of ethical relativism is often misunderstood, and that the issues involved are inextricably bound up with the hermeneutical problems considered in Chapter I. It emerges that the theory of ethics I have advanced is not in any sense relativist; nevertheless, it is unavoidably and desirably pluralist. As a result, it will certainly be the case that to argue along the lines I advocate will lead to a broad range of moral views which cannot easily be compared or contrasted with one another in any direct way. This has immediate and important implications both for our own use of earlier Christian tradition, and for our policy with regard to the teaching of Christianity in cultures other than our own.

The final chapter, by way of a summary, attempts to outline the way in which moral discussion, training and research might be conducted in a Christian community which wholeheartedly adopted the method I have outlined. It is argued that an accurate understanding of the nature of the various authorities to which appeal might be made will, in the end, tend to enhance and not to diminish the status of those authorities. The picture painted in this chapter is, as I am well aware, an idealized one. I have included it here not just because moralists have an inveterate desire to moralize, but because, as I have already said, any theory is in the end commended to our attention by its fruitfulness. If it is true that the approach I am proposing leads in the direction of the kind of Christian moral theology described in this chapter, and if this picture of the Christian moral community is found to be attractive even as an ideal, then my theory as a whole will have the kind of supportive evidence which it needs.

Authority in Morals

'The authority of morals is the authority of truth, that is of reality . . .

'The love which brings the right answer is an exercise of justice and realism and really *looking*.'

Iris Murdoch
The Sovereignty of Good

I

The Authority of Christian Tradition

The ultimate norm for Christian belief is God's revelation of himself in Jesus of Nazareth. The contemporary Christian does not have direct access to the life and teaching of Jesus. Who Jesus was, what he did and the meaning of his life, are mediated to the Christian by the tradition of the Christian community, a tradition which consists both in the living faith handed on from believer to believer, and in the texts, starting with the Bible, in which that faith has found more permanent expression. This tradition is authoritative for Christian belief in that, somehow or other, Christian beliefs are justified in the last analysis by appeal to that tradition. The precise way in which this is done varies in different Christian communities. Some theologians would lay greater stress than others on the Bible, and especially the New Testament, somewhat at the expense of later Christian tradition, while others would wish to regard the tradition as a whole in a more unified way. Others, again, would lay more stress on the experience of the individual believer within the living tradition of the Church. Despite these variations, however, the appeal to tradition as normative for Christian belief is to be found in at any rate all the main Christian communities.

The Christian is well aware that his religious beliefs are such that he is also required to strive for moral perfection. It might well seem natural to him to suppose that the ultimate authority to which appeal is to be made in moral questions is the same tradition to which he appeals in questions of religious belief. It is this view which I shall examine in this chapter. As with questions of religious belief, the appeal to tradition to settle moral questions can take various forms according to whether the emphasis falls on the New Testament, later tradition, or the experience of the individual believer. I shall not examine these differences in detail, since I hope to show that the logic of the argument is the same in each case so far as concerns the points I wish to make.

Two qualifications will be in order. I do not intend to examine the claim that Christians come by their religious beliefs by being brought up in a believing community (which, at least in most cases, is plainly true), and come by their moral beliefs in the same way (which is at least arguable). I am not concerned with the historical, social, and personal factors which are responsible for producing the moral beliefs Christians hold. I am concerned with the way in which these beliefs are to be justified, rather than how they are to be explained. Secondly, I shall not be concerned with those moral duties which would be unintelligible apart from Christian belief as a whole. For example, Christians believe themselves to be obliged to worship God in a particular way, typically, if not in every case, by the celebration of the Eucharist. They consider themselves obliged to ask God's forgiveness for their sins, and to thank him for what he has done for them through his Son. It might be argued that these obligations are better described as religious rather than moral, though I myself would incline to think it clearer to describe them as moral obligations. Be that as it may, they are plainly obligations which would make no sense were it not for the other beliefs which Christians hold on the basis of what God revealed in Christ. I shall be concerned only with those other moral obligations which it would make sense for an unbeliever to consider himself bound by. Thus, any man might consider himself bound to keep promises, to care for his fellow men, to be faithful to his marriage, and even to give his life for others. He might argue that some of these beliefs, especially perhaps the last one, could not in the end be justified. But at least it makes sense to ask whether such beliefs can be justified without appeal to Christian revelation, in a way which would not make sense in the case of, say, the celebration of the Eucharist.

If we ask how these more general moral beliefs are to be justified, or what method is to be followed in trying to discover whether they are true or false, the Christian might adopt one or other of two basic positions. Either he will claim that some (or even all) moral problems must remain insoluble to anyone who does not hold Christian beliefs, or he will refuse to make this claim. And the positive claim might be held in a stronger form, as I have just expressed it, or in the weaker form that although the non-Christian can provide a partial justification for his moral beliefs, he cannot provide an ultimate justification for them. On this weaker view, Christian revelation would be regarded as an essential supplement to, but not as a substitute for, the arguments available to the non-believer.

Both the stronger and the weaker versions of this Christian claim hold that revelation can function as the ultimate court of appeal in moral argument, and that arguments which do not make this appeal will be either wholly or partly deficient. In harmony with this claim, a Christian might well speak of a humanist approach to moral problems in a way which implies that such an approach will be at best incomplete, and at worst will lead to false moral conclusions, precisely because it does not take any theological considerations into account.

I shall argue in the remainder of this chapter that neither the stronger nor the weaker versions of this Christian claim can be upheld consistently with other Christian beliefs about God. And I shall supplement this purely theological argument by advancing further philosophical considerations which tell against the truth of any such claim. The aims of this chapter are thus entirely negative. Nevertheless, I believe it is the right place to start, firstly because the view that I criticize here is perhaps the one which would naturally occur to the Christian, and is one which is reinforced by the habit of referring to 'the Christian ethic'; and secondly because it prepares the ground for my own positive suggestions in the following chapters. I should also like to stress that I am endeavouring to disprove only the claim that Christian revelation functions as the *ultimate* court of appeal in morals. There may be (and, as I shall later argue, there are) other ways in which Christian tradition can be used in ethics. These uses are left wholly untouched by the arguments in this chapter.

Morality and the Will of God

Any Christian would hold that what ought to be done in any situation is also what God wills should be done, for to deny this would imply that the Christian believes in a God who is, at best, unconcerned with our moral behaviour. The whole Judaeo-Christian tradition is clear that such a God is not the one in whom they believe. The Judaeo-Christian God reveals himself as a God who is most deeply concerned that his followers be just, pure, forgiving, honest, and loving. For the Christian, then, to be morally good is also to do the will of God; and to do the will of God is also to be morally good. The notions of 'moral duty' and 'what God wills us to do' are, in short, materially equivalent. Any instance of the one will also be an instance of the other.

That two terms are materially equivalent does not necessarily mean that one can be defined in terms of the other. For example, it may be the case that anyone who is a British citizen in good standing over the age of eighteen is also one who is eligible to vote in a British election. But 'eligible to vote in a British election' does not *mean* 'British citizen in good standing over the age of eighteen'. Thus, from the fact that 'what God wills us to do' and 'moral duty' are materially equivalent expressions for the Christian, we cannot conclude that 'moral duty' *means* 'what God wills us to do'. To hold that the two expressions are definitionally equivalent in this way is to be forced onto the horns of a most uncomfortable dilemma. On the one hand, we might have to admit that 'moral duty' is to be defined in terms of the will of God because things become our moral duty only as a result of God's willing that they should be; and this is in the end a thoroughgoing voluntarist position. Alternatively, we might have to admit that 'moral duty' is to be defined in terms of God's will for us because we, with our limited human understanding, are unable to give any other content to the notion of 'moral duty'. I shall examine, and reject, each alternative in turn.

What precisely would be the difficulty in adopting a voluntarist position? After all, there is surely a sense in which it is true that moral values and moral duties do depend on the will of God to create human beings. Had he chosen to create some other type of moral being, would not that have entailed willing them to have a different morality? Even on a Kantian view, in which morality applies to all rational agents as such, it would, I think follow that different species of moral agents would have a morality different in its content, though not in its form, from the moralities of other species. In this sense, then, it is part of Christian belief that the morality we have is what it is because of God's decision so to create us. The distinctive, and objectionable, contention of the voluntarist is that, even given the creation of man, what is right and wrong for men to do depends on a *further* act of God's will; God could have placed us under different, incompatible, obligations while leaving us unaltered. In thus severing the connection between the nature of man and the moral obligations under which God could place him, the voluntarist renders man's moral perfection unintelligible, because it is no longer related to any other facet of man's development. He therefore runs the risk of making his God arbitrary. In the main, Christian tradition has rejected this picture of God as inconsistent with his character as it has been revealed to us and with the ways in which his moral concern for us has been shown.

The other horn of the dilemma is hardly more attractive. The argument would have to run something like this: although it is of course true that God is not arbitrary in himself, and that he must have his reasons for deciding that we should be subject to certain moral obligations rather than others, nevertheless we are not in a position to know what those reasons might be. Our knowledge of ourselves might be so inadequate that we cannot grasp the relationship between what God wills us to do and the good that will result for us if we obey him. God's purposes are, after all, ultimately mysterious.

This argument does not suffice to rescue God from the charge of arbitrariness. So far as *we* are concerned, the God depicted in this argument would be indistinguishable from the God of the full-blooded voluntarist. If we can see no connection between our human fulfilment and the obligations under which God places us, then we would have no grounds for believing that our God was a moral God at all. To be sure, he might tell us that he was; but why should we believe him? Not because of his mighty deeds. Mighty deeds are no more than displays of power, and power can be misused, or can exist without any moral dimension to it whatever. Volcanoes and master criminals might both be capable of displaying great power; but they lack altogether the moral seriousness which, according to Christian tradition, we must find in God if we are to be able to recognize him *as* God. It appears that there are strong theological reasons against the view that we can never understand God's reasons for obliging us as he does, quite apart from the fact that such a view would make nonsense of our attempts to think about morality in a coherent way.

There are other equally serious difficulties against this type of position. For it to work in practice, two conditions would have to be met; firstly, it would have to be possible for us to come to know what God wills for us; secondly, it would have to be the case that, independently of what God tells us about our moral obligations, we could have no access to the basis of ethics such as, for example, a knowledge of our own nature might provide. Thus it might be the case that God's will for us was based on an anthropology which he revealed to us only in Christ, in comparison with which our own efforts to formulate an anthropology independently of revelation would be either totally false or too misleading to function as a foundation for ethics. Are there any grounds for believing that such is indeed our situation?

We may begin by inquiring what theological grounds might be urged in favour of the view that, independently of what God tells us about our moral obligations, we could have no access to the basis of ethics. At least in some passages, Karl Barth seems to come close to this kind of view.[1] A full discussion of this position is not possible here, but it appears in the end to rest on two main lines of argument, both stemming from an analysis of original sin.

The first line of argument asserts that as a result of original sin our minds are too clouded in darkness, too blinded, to be able to think properly about morality. The difficulty with this assertion, I think, lies not so much in the assertion itself, although even here there is the hint of a certain self-defeating quality about it. The main difficulty comes when it is combined with other assertions

---

[1]   Barth, ch.8, pp. 509–732. References in footnotes are to the bibliography at the end of the book. The bibliography for each chapter is arranged alphabetically by author.

which the Christian would also wish to make, such as the assertion that man's mind is capable of responding to God's revelation when it is offered to us. It might be argued, perhaps, that we are able to accept revelation as true only by the grace of God, and that faith itself is a gift. But if grace is able to help in this case, why could it not have helped in the first place? To this in turn it might be replied that it is Christ who alone is God's grace for us, and that grace is therefore given only in connection with the response to Christ. However, I should have thought it by now a fairly well-established theological position that all men, by virtue of their being created in Christ, have grace offered to them, whether or not they ever have the opportunity to respond to revelation as such.

The rebuttal of this line of argument, then, does not depend on a kind of Pelagian position to the effect that, despite original sin, man is perfectly capable of working out his moral obligations by the light of his natural, ungraced, reason alone. I can see little theological merit in the view that there ever in fact exists such a thing as a natural reason alone, outside the order of grace. Unfortunately, the use of the term 'natural' in speaking of natural law morality has given the impression that 'natural' is to be contrasted with 'supernatural' or 'graced', and that a natural law morality is therefore a morality in which God and his grace are in no way involved. I see no reason for the Christian theologian to make this contrast, and every reason why he should not. The real focus of the discussion should not be on fallen man without grace, but rather on sinful man without explicit belief in the Christian revelation.

If we manage to remain clear on this point, I think a great deal of the force of this first line of argument from the reality of original sin is lost. Even were one to accept that the effect of original sin was totally to blind our minds to our true nature and destiny (and at least Catholic theologians would probably not accept even so much), we would have to remember that precisely because Christ died for all men we are *not* left simply with our unaided sinful minds when we come to consider morality. The grace of Christ is offered to us, even if the opportunity for explicit Christian belief is not. One would therefore require very strong *additional* arguments to show that our minds are still incapable of correct ethical reflection unless they also come to accept the teaching of the New

Testament as the Word of God. Moreover, it is far from clear how any alleged revelation could possibly commend itself to us as truly God's revelation were it to appear to us to have immoral implications. Revelation commends itself to us in part because it does harmonize with our moral aspirations. It follows that those moral aspirations must have been present antecedently (at least in a logical sense). I conclude, then, that the Christian theologian must hold not, indeed, that man has the ability to understand morality independently of God's grace, but rather that he has that ability independently of his coming to believe in Christ on the basis of God's revelation.

The same general reply is sufficient, I think, to meet the second line of argument drawn from the doctrine of original sin. On this line, it might well be conceded that man (fallen man with the help of grace, that is) has the intellectual capacity to discover and assent to moral truths; but it might be urged that he will still be seriously misled if he uses this capacity to reflect upon himself, because the desires and aspirations of his human nature are also warped by the effects of original sin. That human desires as they actually are offer no firm basis for ethics is a view with a long and distinguished history, stretching back to the Augustinian interpretation of the Fall and, behind him, to the Platonic distrust of the body in which our soul is imprisoned. One still occasionally hears echoes of the confused asceticism which speaks of the need to replace purely natural desires by supernatural ones (thus repeating the equivocation on the word 'natural' to which I have already called attention). A full philosophical critique of the place of desires in ethics will be offered in the next chapter; but I shall anticipate some of my remarks there in order to place them here in a more theological setting.

I know of no moral philosopher who has ever maintained that living morally requires us to satisfy any and every desire that we might have. For a start, many of our desires conflict with one another, so that it is not possible in practice to satisfy them all. Furthermore, it would be widely if not universally admitted that some of our desires are irrational, or open to criticism on some other score, and that living morally requires us to forego their satisfaction in order to satisfy others. Still, even admitting all that, one might maintain that it is the desires we have which, in some fashion or other, must provide the basis of our morality, and that it simply would not make sense to say that the first step in moral thinking consists in recognizing that *all* our desires are warped, that we do not know how they are warped, and that our morality must therefore take no account of them whatever. Suppose, however, that we were to hold such a position in its extreme form. One could then easily see how the theologian could use it to argue for the absolute necessity of revelation for ethics.

But consider how revelation would strike us in such a situation. Were it the case that our desires were warped and that we could not, of ourselves, see in what way they were warped, then any alleged revelation of our moral duty would appear to us arbitrary, dehumanizing, and, ultimately, voluntarist. It would be quite unreasonable to accept such a revelation as authentic. In short, this view leads straight back to the full-blooded voluntarist position which I have already criticised. Moreover, I think it would also present a picture of a God who is most unreasonably demanding in the light of what we are able to accomplish in our fallen state. It is surely part of our normal moral view that we should not have quite unrealistic expectations of people, and that we should not place burdens upon them which they are simply incapable of bearing. On the view I am here criticizing, God must inevitably appear as demanding of us that we should live in a way which frustrates all the desires we actually have. No doubt it might be said that the point of a revealed ethic is that we should stand condemned and recognize our need of God's healing power; and, at a pinch, I can see the possibility and the value of God's revealing to us the moral dimension of life in his Kingdom even if it corresponds little or not at all to our present fallen desires and aspirations. But the point of doing Christian ethics is to try to determine how we should live here and now, as we are, in our imperfect and fallen world. It is one thing to be told that our present desires have nothing to do with the morality of the Kingdom to come (though, like Kant, I could not believe even that much); it is very much worse to be told that our present desires have nothing to do with how we ought to live here and now. A God who said *that* would be so lacking in understanding and compassion that we could have little reason to believe in him.

Up to this point, I have been arguing against the view that there are theological grounds for saying that we have no secure basis for ethics independently of revelation. In the end, my argument turns on the contention that belief in revelation is irrational unless that revelation somehow fits in with our antecedent convictions, and, in particular, with our antecedent moral convictions. This general view, commonly held by Catholic theologians, has often enough seemed Pelagian, at least in its implications, to many theologians in the Reformed traditions, and they might still incline to this view despite my efforts to show the difficulties involved in holding it consistently. Indeed, even in the Catholic tradition there are some moral theologians who hold in practice, if not in theory, that revelation is essential for our understanding of ethics. For instance, it is not uncommon to find Catholic theologians arguing that there are no conclusive arguments against the legitimacy of divorce and remarriage unless one appeals to the New Testament teaching on the subject and to the traditional interpretation of that teaching by the Church. Sometimes, though less often, a similar position is adopted with regard to suicide, or the laying down of one's life for others. The same kind of view is implied, I believe, by any position which holds that there is a specifically Christian ethic, the conclusions of which cannot be firmly established without appeal to revelation and the tradition of the Church guided by the Holy Spirit. In my view, this position is inconsistent with the basic rationalism which underpins the whole Catholic tradition in theology, and I hope to have shown that it presents enormous difficulties for any Christian theologian. Be that as it may, however, to establish the position that revelation is the ultimate basis of Christian ethics it is not enough to show that attempts to find an alternative basis are theologically unsound. Someone who disagrees with my arguments thus far would still have established only half of his case. As I point out above (page 6), it would also be necessary to show that revelation *can* provide the ultimate basis for ethics which cannot be found elsewhere, and that appeal to revelation will enable us to solve moral dilemmas to which there is no other adequate solution. I shall now attempt to prove that this part of the case cannot be substantiated either.

The Appeal to Biblical Tradition

The attempt to appeal to biblical tradition as the ultimate authority in ethics runs into several difficulties, which may be conveniently labelled exegetical, hermeneutical, and theological. I shall discuss each of these in turn.

Exegetical difficulties

Fundamental to any proper use of the Bible is a respect for the nature of the biblical text. That means, in general, not merely that we must respect the basic Christian belief that it is inspired by God; we must also recognize the fact that the documents it contains are thoroughly human documents, written at a particular time and place with the requirements of a particular readership in mind. The fact that the biblical texts are human documents makes it at once possible, and difficult, for us to discern in them what it is that God wishes us to learn.

Any ancient culture is, and must to some extent remain, opaque to us. In particular, its language will be only imperfectly understood, and the precise flavour and overtones of its expressions may well escape us even when we are superficially able to give verbal equivalents of all its utterances. Even with a contemporary European language, it is often very difficult indeed to capture in English exactly what is being said, no matter how many dictionaries and native speakers we have at our disposal. Sometimes, indeed, there simply *is* no way of saying in English precisely what is being clearly said in the foreign language.

There are two different types of problems involved. The first is the problem of mastering a foreign language. This involves attaining a grasp of the many conventions governing the use of words, expressions, and literary forms, as well as many other conventions regarding tone of voice, context and circumstances, all of which can determine the meaning of what is said. Thus, for me to understand another English-speaker, I must know the rules governing the use of the words he employs; I must know to what words like 'table' or 'chair' or 'shyness' refer; I must also know how to determine whether 'Angela sailed into Portsmouth in great style' is to be taken metaphorically or literally; I must also be able to tell whether 'John knows everything' is to be taken as a straight assertion or as a sarcastic criticism. In the case of written texts, I must know how to tell whether *Animal Farm* is a children's story or a political satire, and whether a poem is just about the changing seasons or is also about the shifting patterns of human feelings. All these points depend on the various conventions which English-speakers employ in communicating with one another. In the case of an ancient language, the evidence upon which our understanding of these conventions is based may be inadequate, or, on occasion, simply non-existent.

Secondly, it may well be the case that a written sentence, or even a series of sentences, could be ambiguous as it stands, but be quite unambiguous when spoken or written on a particular occasion. Thus, even in English, the sentence 'England collapse before Australian attack' could refer to cricket, or to a military disaster; but the same sentence written on a sports' page of a newspaper could have only one meaning. By the same token, our understanding of an ancient text will depend on the amount of evidence at our disposal about the occasion and circumstances in which it was originally uttered. This evidence, too, may be seriously incomplete.

Examples of difficulties of both these kinds are not hard to find in the New Testament generally, and in New Testament ethics in particular. Kierkegaard once attacked New Testament scholars for refusing to translate *misein* as 'hate' in the saying about 'hating one's father and mother', and wished to insist that the word be taken in its full literal sense.[2] Scholars are still not entirely clear about what is meant by *porneia* in the exception-clause to the divorce-saying in Matthew's gospel.[3] We find it hard, on occasions, to be sure whether a contemporary would have understood that a particular saying was meant literally or as a rhetorical exaggeration. We may be fairly sure about being told to cut off a hand, or pluck out an eye, if these are sources of scandal to us – though Kierkegaard might once again accuse us of watering down the clear meaning just because we find it intolerable. But are we so sure whether the command not to resist one who is evil is to be taken

---

[2] Kierkegaard, pp. 103–109.   [3] E.g. most recently, Fitzmeyer.

as a practical guide to our behaviour in the face of aggression? And is it not said in the same style, and in the same context, as the commands never to use any oath whatever, and not to get divorced and remarry? Does Luke's gospel mean to say that in order to be a disciple a rich man must sell everything that he has? Does John's gospel teach only that we must love our fellow-Christians, and not our enemies? Does Matthew's gospel require us to keep every jot and tittle of the Law of Moses? These are matters of literary convention and usage, and for many of them we simply have insufficient evidence to be sure of the answer.

In short, we are simply at too great a remove from the texts to be entirely confident that we have understood them correctly. After all, it is only in comparatively recent times that Christians (and even now, not all Christians) have recognized that the author of Genesis was not describing the process of creation. And theologians who would never dream of taking a literalist view of Genesis I, Jonah, or Mark 13, are still perfectly capable of being quite uncritical when it comes to New Testament ethics (or, for that matter, New Testament accounts of miracles). Fundamentalism, which in the end tries to deny that exegetical problems exist, still dies hard.

The claim that the biblical tradition can function as the ultimate court of appeal in ethics would be somewhat more plausible were it the case that we could always guarantee to have properly understood the New Testament text. In fact, no such guarantee is available. And even if it were, it is quite obvious that the New Testament simply does not consider many of the moral problems with which we are faced. It is silent on the development of nuclear power stations, genetic engineering, birth control, organ transplants, and the moral dilemmas arising directly from the industrial revolution and the rise of modern capitalism. It says nothing about the proper ownership of the means of production. To be sure, texts can be found teaching that we must love others as we do ourselves, and that those are blessed who hunger and thirst after justice, or who practise the corporal works of mercy. But none of these texts will suffice as an ultimate court of appeal to settle all our ethical problems.

Hermeneutical difficulties

Whereas exegetical problems are concerned with understanding the text, I take hermeneutical problems to be concerned with its application. Once again, the analogy with language is helpful.

Mastering a foreign language is one thing, translating it into one's own is quite another, bringing with it a new set of difficulties. Sometimes, as perhaps with the German word *Gemütlichkeit*, there may simply be no synonym in English. Sometimes, there may be an equivalent but not strictly a synonym; for example, it may be that a Spanish proverb to the effect that one cannot both toll the bells and walk in the procession is roughly an equivalent of what we (more earthy and less spiritual?) English mean by 'You can't have your cake and eat it'. Again, we may be deceived by etymological similarity into assuming that we have found a synonym when we have not, as when a schoolboy takes Virgil to have described Aeneas as pious. I think that the same kind of problem arises when we try to identify in one culture an action or a situation which is the same as one in another culture — a problem on which I shall have something more to say in Chapter IV. Quine has, I believe, shown convincingly that problems of synonymy cannot be solved in any very simple way.[4] Though I would not subscribe to his more radical conclusions which might suggest that translation is always, and ineradicably, indeterminate, and that we might have no means of deciding between different incompatible translations, I do think he has shown that we cannot decide between them just on the evidence internal to the text itself. Assumptions have to be made which cannot of themselves be justified on the evidence of the text.

The importance of these considerations for the use of the biblical tradition as an authority in ethics is very considerable. In particular, I think it can be shown that in order to understand the import of New Testament ethics (even assuming that the exegetical problems have been successfully overcome) for the moral problems of our own day, specifically *moral* assumptions must be made which cannot themselves be justified from within the New Testament text itself. It cannot be taken for granted, and cannot be proved from

[4] Quine, ch. 2, esp. pp. 73—9.

the text alone, that we have found correct synonyms for the moral words which they contain, nor that we have correctly identified in our own culture the problems and situations which correspond to the problems and situations dealt with in the ethical passages in the New Testament. There are serious problems in transferring New Testament solutions straight into our own day and cultures; and these problems become quite insoluble in principle if (as is implied by the view that the New Testament is the only ultimate court of appeal) we are forbidden to make any moral assumptions not already given in the text.

Some examples may be helpful at this point. Jesus himself, and most if not all the New Testament writers, developed their teaching on marriage in the context of monogamous cultures. There is no automatic way of deciding, from this teaching alone, what they would have said in a polygamous society. Again, Jesus referred to the practice of divorce in earlier Israelite tradition and ascribed it to the necessity created by the hardness of heart of the people in question. He taught a very much stricter doctrine to his disciples. From the text alone, it remains an open question what he would have said had he been speaking to us. Similarly, it does not automatically follow that Paul would have told 19th-century plantation workers in Mississippi to be obedient to their masters, and been content simply to leave it at that, just because he was willing to take that line with the slaves of the Roman Empire. It does not automatically follow that the position of women with regard to their husbands or to their position in the Christian community should automatically remain in our day as it was at the time Paul was writing his letters. It may even be that certain elements of New Testament ethics were written in the belief that the world was shortly to come to an end. Such an *Interimsethik*, obviously, need not still apply to us who no longer share that belief.

In order even to begin to deal with questions like 'What would Jesus (or Paul, or whoever) have said on this topic had he been speaking to Christians of our own day?', we have to have some way of determining which differences between New Testament times and our own are significant, and which are not. Thus, we might conclude that the differences between having several wives in contemporary West Africa and having several wives in 1st-century

Palestine are important, and that the New Testament teaching on marriage would have to be expressed very differently in contemporary West African cultures. We might be of the opinion that slavery in the Roman Empire was so different from slavery as practised in 19th-century Mississippi that Paul could not possibly simply have enjoined obedience on the plantation workers. We might notice that the early Church took a very liberal line when faced with the problems of 'translating' Jewish Christianity into a Gentile Greek culture, at least so far as the observance of the Mosaic Law was concerned. But even that will not suffice to prove that equally liberal solutions can be applied to the other problems I have mentioned, unless it is also proved that those problems are comparable in the relevant respects to the problems facing Paul on his missionary journeys.

Now, it is plain that the New Testament texts nowhere set out any method of deciding which circumstances are morally significant and which are not. They do not always, or even usually, set out which features of the contemporary problem were taken to be significant by the writers themselves. To decide which differences are, and which are not, significant demands further moral reflection which, without vicious circularity, cannot itself be based on the authority of the New Testament. In short, it demands the exercise of our own independent moral reasoning, no doubt assisted by grace. It is thus wholly misleading to suggest that the biblical tradition can be appealed to as the ultimate authority in ethics over and against our own moral reasoning, or that our own moral reasoning must itself be based on revelation as it is transmitted by the New Testament texts. The suggestion that, in contrast to the obscurity or futility of our own moral reasoning, we have clear and independent access to the revealed will of God in the biblical texts totally ignores the most elementary pitfalls of interpretation. Even the briefest consideration of the problems of hermeneutics makes it clear that the application of the New Testament to our own ethical problems would be quite impossible in default of other moral assumptions which could be defended on independent grounds. It follows that the authority of the biblical tradition cannot, for us, be ultimate.

Theological difficulties

In a much more tentative way, I wish to raise a third kind of difficulty against the appeal to the New Testament as the ultimate authority in ethics. Although this difficulty is of central importance, it does not seem to me to have received the attention it deserves. I am not myself at all sure about the grounds on which it might be settled, and must content myself with an account of the issues as I see them, in the hope that others can take the matter further.

The Second Vatican Council taught that the books of the Bible are inspired, and therefore inerrant, concerning 'that truth which God wanted put into the sacred writings for the sake of our salvation'.[5] This is not, of course, to say that some passages of the Bible are inspired and others are not, but rather to say that in every passage we must try to discern what that truth is which God wished to be expressed there for the sake of our salvation. Now, it would be generally agreed that assertions about physics or astronomy or geography or history are not in themselves and as such instances of what I shall briefly term 'salvation-truths', although they may well be made in the course of attempts by the biblical writers to communicate salvation-truths. I wish, then, to raise the question about the status of statements in the Bible about ethics.

It seems at first sight natural enough to assume that ethics is much more intimately connected with salvation than is physics or astronomy, and to conclude from this that the ethical assertions in the Bible fall under the category of teaching which is inspired and therefore inerrant. After all, as I have argued above, it is a salient characteristic of the God of the Judaeo-Christian tradition that he is morally concerned about this world, and that the response he asks for from his followers is, in part, a moral response. He does not necessarily require us to be good physicists, but he does require us to be good men.

This position is traditional, and, to my knowledge, has never been seriously challenged. It may well be correct. Still, I believe that some questions can be raised about it which need to be satisfactorily answered before the traditional position can be maintained without hesitation.

[5] *Dei Verbum*, III, 11.

In the first place, it is clearly not traditional Christian teaching that we must all be in possession of correct answers to all our moral problems in order to be saved. If such were the case, we might also have expected the biblical writers, especially the New Testament writers, to exhibit a much greater urgency than they do about the whole range of moral problems. In fact, the impression their writings give is that morality is for the most part not their first concern, and that when they do consider moral issues it is usually because these issues have caused controversy or division in the Christian community. Occasionally, too, as in the case of Paul's teaching on the eating of meat offered to idols, the moral issue has immediate dogmatic implications. But there is in the New Testament as a whole no systematic attempt at a complete moral teaching, and little sign that the writers felt that it was particularly important that they should provide such teaching.

Moreover, it is worth looking carefully at the way in which moral issues are introduced into the New Testament writings. The impression is quite clearly given that the writers expect the Christian to take moral issues seriously. They insist that moral seriousness is a condition for entry into the Kingdom, although each individual writer tends to have his own particular emphasis on what such moral seriousness will involve. It seems to me, then, clearly to be a salvation-truth that God requires us to be morally good, and to make serious efforts to become so. Furthermore, it seems to me clearly false to say that God requires us never to make a mistake about what we ought to do. The crucial question, then, is this: are particular teachings on particular moral issues taught as salvation-truths, or are they offered simply because it is in general a salvation-truth that to take such issues seriously is required of us by our Christian belief? More detailed argument than I have seen seems to me to be required to establish that the individual moral assertions in the New Testament are salvation-truths rather than the opinions of the writers offered in the course of reinforcing the general truth that our moral behaviour is intimately connected with the Kingdom. In short, I would welcome attempts to spell out in detail the traditional position that revelation is concerned with the details of morality, and not just with the general importance of being morally good. Unless this is done satisfactorily, the question of using revelation as the ultimate authority in ethics simply does not arise at all.

This issue is independent of the argument of the two preceding sections, which may now be briefly summarized. The appeal to biblical tradition as ultimately authoritative in contrast to the uncertainty or impossibility of alternative groundings for ethics cannot be justified, just because of the very nature of that tradition itself. Firstly, the biblical writings simply do not contain solutions to most of our moral problems; secondly, the evidence at our disposal for understanding the meaning of the biblical writings is not in every case adequate; thirdly, and most important of all, the process of interpreting the biblical tradition in terms which are applicable to our culture and circumstances is one which demands that further moral assumptions be made for which the text itself cannot provide any justification. This hermeneutical problem is quite a general one, and does not apply only to ethics, but to the interpretation and translation of any text from a different language or culture. Hence, the attempt to use the biblical tradition as ultimately authoritative is viciously circular, since it must invoke precisely those processes of independent moral reasoning which it is the purpose of the attempt to circumvent.

The Appeal to Subsequent Christian Tradition

I shall be dealing with the legitimate appeal to the authority of the Christian tradition, and in particular with the problems connected with infallibility in morals, at much greater length in Chapter IV. Here I wish to consider a much more limited point. Can it be argued that the difficulties encountered in the above discussion of the biblical tradition can be overcome by appeal to subsequent tradition, and in particular by appeal to the texts in which its moral views and its interpretation of the biblical texts are expressed? It might be thought, for instance, that if we believe in the guidance of the Holy Spirit in the Church, especially if we consider the strong form of this belief in the Catholic tradition, any questions we might have about the meaning and interpretation of the biblical tradition and its applicability to our own day could be resolved by considering the way it has been understood and used by the Church throughout its history.

I do not think that this position can be maintained. There is a general reason why we should not expect it to be true. Even on the 'highest' view of the guidance of the Spirit in the Church, this guidance will not be any stronger than that given by the Spirit to the inspired writers (if I may use the phrase as a convenient shorthand) of the biblical texts. If the fact that the biblical texts are inspired does not remove all our difficulties about the meaning and application of those texts to our own day, I do not see how the guidance of the Spirit in the Church will remove our difficulties in understanding and applying the documents of Christian tradition.

More specifically, the documents of Christian tradition present precisely the same problems as the biblical writings. We believe that they continue to hand down to us the revelation which God gave us in his Son. They do this by the very fact that they are the reflections of men, guided by the Spirit, on the events of the life of Jesus and on the earlier tradition in which those events were first reflected upon and interpreted. It follows that to arrive at a precise understanding of the meaning of these documents requires a study of the context, conventions, idiom, and presuppositions of their authors. This purely exegetical task is far from easy. Moreover, we are well aware that the documents of the Christian tradition are influenced also by all too human considerations. Their authors were men of their times, subject to the prejudices, cultural limitations and moral fashions of their age. Frequently, too, they had to labour under the handicap of an inadequate exegetical method so far as their interpretation of the biblical writings was concerned. Their arguments may be hard for us to grasp because they are couched in terms of philosophical positions which we might find unhelpful or confused. I myself, for instance, would not share Augustine's Platonism nor the moral and ascetical conclusions which follow from it; and although I would be much more in sympathy with Aquinas's Aristotelian approach to ethics, I feel that he, too, has been misunderstood and misrepresented by many moralists in the last hundred years or so. And in any event, Platonism, Aristotelianism, or linguistic analysis are not God's revelation. For all these reasons, it is plain that the documents of later Christian tradition will both communicate and obscure God's revelation from our point of view.

Hence, just as in the case of the biblical writings, we have the hermeneutical problem of knowing just how their authors would have expressed themselves had they been writing for us, confronted with our problems and our situation. Would they still have condemned the lending of money at interest? Would they still consider it possible to meet the conditions for a just war? Would they still have been unsympathetic to democratic forms of government? Would they still have been willing to consider abortion less reprehensible at an early stage in pregnancy? Once again, the point at issue is not directly to answer these questions one way or the other; the point is that in order to justify any answer, we need additional moral arguments, over and above the mere fact that certain views were taught at a particular time and place, or that they were generally accepted by the Christians at that time. These additional moral arguments cannot themselves, without vicious circularity, consist in further appeals to tradition. Fundamentalism with regard to subsequent Christian tradition is just as untenable, for the same reasons, as is fundamentalism with regard to the biblical writings themselves. It follows that tradition cannot legitimately be considered as the ultimate authority in ethics, or as a way of avoiding the necessity for the ordinary processes of moral reasoning.

The Appeal to Personal Revelation

A discussion of the appeal to personal revelation in a chapter about the authority of Christian tradition might seem to be something of a digression. On the other hand, there are some Christian traditions where stress is laid on the personal relationship between the believer and God, and in which it is held that it is in this relationship alone that God's will is ultimately revealed. Several current discussions of Christian ethics seem to presuppose a view of this kind. In any event, it comes here in the argument, since I believe that it raises just the same kinds of issues as those we have already been considering.

The position I wish to criticize represents yet another attempt to appeal to revelation to the exclusion of ordinary moral reasoning, and relies for its theological underpinning upon the Christian belief that the Spirit is present in all believers, prompting and guiding them in their Christian vocation. This position is often reinforced, for example in Brunner[6] and to some extent in Bultmann,[7] by appeal to the biblical teaching on the New Law, or, as in some passages of Rahner,[8] by the view that discernment of spirits is to be the distinctively Christian method of deciding where our vocation lies, in contrast to the ordinary process of moral reasoning through universal principles.

The classical exposition of this view is to be found in Kierkegaard's *Fear and Trembling*. Kierkegaard considers the dilemma facing Abraham when he was called upon by God to sacrifice his son Isaac, and uses this biblical story to illustrate what he takes to be a fundamental point in Christian ethics. Kierkegaard is perfectly clear that ordinary moral reasoning would unequivocally condemn as murder the sacrifice of one's own son. But he points out that Abraham's dilemma is not that of the ordinary tragic hero, caught between conflicting moral obligations. In Abraham's case, the conflict is between morality and his duty towards God. The ethical code in which Abraham believes is precisely the source of his temptation, which Abraham can overcome only by a supreme act of faith. In his personal relationship to God in faith Abraham can see that he has a duty to transcend ordinary moral reasoning in order to do God's will. God's call to him is, in the depths of their personal relationship, self-authenticating. Abraham's greatness consists in his willingness to respond to this personal revelation of God in defiance of his ordinary moral convictions.

The logic of this position is the same as that of the two views we have already examined. It is assumed that there are some dilemmas about what we ought to do (Kierkegaard could not, for the reason just given, describe them as *moral* dilemmas) which cannot be correctly solved by the application of ordinary moral reasoning, and which are resolved only in the light of revelation. God's will cannot be reliably discovered by moral argument, but, at least in some cases, only when God explicitly discloses himself,

---

6   Brunner, pp. 78–93.   7   Bultmann, ch. 3.
8   Rahner, and the reply by Dorr.

revealing man's true destiny as he revealed Abraham's.

The problem with Kierkegaard's position, as with any position which stresses the uniqueness of the vocation of the individual Christian, is that it proves far too much, and in so doing proves nothing at all. One major check on any alleged revelation is, as I have argued above, our ordinary moral convictions. Once this check is removed, it is hard to see any reliable way of distinguishing between genuine revelations of God's will and sincere but mistaken personal convictions. If the vocation of the individual Christian is unique, then, *ex hypothesi,* there is nothing that can be said *in principle* about how he ought to live, and no way of showing that *any* decision he feels called upon to make, however outlandish it might appear to us, is not part of his unique vocation from God. Once we are asked to believe that God could will even the sacrifice of one's son as a test of faith, running counter to our deepest moral convictions, there is no limit to what such a God might not require. We are but a short step from the fully voluntarist picture of God which was rejected at the beginning of this chapter. I think this is the inevitable conclusion of locating authority ultimately in revelation rather than in the ordinary process of moral reasoning whose authority is logically prior to the acceptance and interpretation of any revelation.

Conclusion

We are now in a position to sum up the arguments of this chapter as a whole. Throughout, I have been arguing against the position that Christian tradition can properly be taken as the *ultimate* authoritative court of appeal in Christian ethics. I have not considered as yet other ways in which the appeal to Christian tradition might be made, or other ways in which its authority might be understood.

I have argued that it is not necessary to take revelation as ultimately authoritative just in order to avoid the Pelagian view that fallen man is perfectly capable of responding to God on his own initiative. The proponent of a natural law theory of ethics, and indeed any Christian moral philosopher, has no need to claim that his moral reflections take place independently of God and his grace. His claim is simply that his moral theory does not ultimately depend upon knowledge of the way in which God has revealed himself in Christ, as that knowledge is mediated to us by the tradition of Christian belief.

I have argued further that a correct understanding of the nature of Christian tradition, whether in the Bible or in later writings, makes it clear that this tradition cannot be ultimately authoritative for our moral reasoning. The documents of this tradition are not simply limpid expressions of the mind of God immediately accessible to all men at all times. God's revelation of himself is not fundamentally a set of utterances, but the person of his Son. The documents of tradition are interpretations of that basic revelation made by human beings under the inspiration and guidance of God, for particular audiences at particular times in history. To discover through them what God is saying to *us* in Christ, we must respond to them with our limited human minds, and with the normal means God places at our disposal. So far as morality is concerned, this response must inevitably include moral reflection which is not in turn dependent on the revelation it is trying to interpret. This moral reflection is epistemologically prior to our appeal to revelation, which cannot therefore be ultimately authoritative. To deny this is to be either voluntarist or fundamentalist or both, and, to that extent, is to subvert both the Christian picture of God and the Christian view of the human context in which he makes himself known.

The conclusion of this argument is not that the Christian moralist should not at any point consider the moral teaching of Christian tradition, nor that this tradition should in no way function as an authority for him. I believe it should (at least provided that there are good grounds for the belief that Christian revelation does contain ethical teaching), and I shall try in Chapters IV and V to say in what sense I believe this to be so. The conclusion is rather that an independent morality is an essential tool in interpreting Christian tradition, since it enables us to distinguish the voice of God from the human voices through which he speaks to us in the tradition of the Church. To the extent that we do succeed in discovering in the tradition of the Church what God is saying to us, we shall do so by the patient methods of moral philosophy which enabled us to hear him in the first place.

I have argued, finally, that there are no good theological reasons for supposing that reflection on our human nature cannot enable us to arrive at moral truth. In particular, the Christian doctrine of original sin should not be understood in a way which makes moral reflection impossible, or in some way inherently misleading. On the other hand, although I have, as I believe, shown the necessity for independent moral reflection if there is to be a Christian ethics, I have as yet given no account of how such reflection might proceed, and on what grounds it might ultimately be based if its ultimate basis is not to be the teaching of Christian tradition. To this more positive task I now turn.

II

The Authority of the Facts

Natural Law Theories

The most radical alternative in Christian ethics to the kinds of theories considered in the last chapter is to be found in the doctrines of the natural law theory of ethics. It should be clear by now that 'natural' here is to be contrasted not with 'supernatural' but with 'revealed in Christ', and that natural law theories should not be regarded by theologians as in any sense a revival of Pelagianism. It is my intention in this chapter to attempt to rehabilitate to some extent the natural law approach to ethics. Any such rehabilitation must, in my view, start from the recognition that there are very many theories which might reasonably be described as 'natural law' theories, even if we restrict our consideration to theories of ethics in the narrow sense, and say nothing of various views about the philosophical basis of civil, criminal, and international law. Indeed, with the possible exception of Kant (and perhaps even he should not be altogether excluded), it is hard to think of a single classical moral philosopher from Aristotle to Hobbes, Locke, Hume, Bentham and Mill, who could not be said to have espoused some version of a natural law theory. Of course these philosophers differ very widely in their views of ethics. But they are at one, I think, in holding that both the content and the form of moral thinking must in the end be derived from an examination of the kind of being man is; and they are also at one in holding that this examination must be conducted by the methods of rational inquiry which we employ also in other, non-moral, fields. The essence of a natural-law theory of morality lies in what it has to say about the starting point and the method of moral thinking. The variety of such theories derive from the different pictures of man which they use as their starting point.

Philosophical criticisms of such theories by Moore and by subsequent British and American philosophers will have to be met in the course of the argument presented in this chapter. As a preliminary, however, I wish to consider two lines of objection which have been advanced primarily in Christian theological circles, which may conveniently be labelled the 'radical' and the 'conservative' objections, respectively.

The radical objection against natural law theories starts from a criticism of many of the conclusions reached by natural law moralists, especially as represented by many Catholic moral theologians. Their arguments have often seemed to be of dubious validity and have given the impression of failing to come to grips with many important contemporary problems in a way that carries conviction. Natural law theory has thus been an easy prey to the criticisms of existentialist philosophers, who, whatever criticisms might in turn be levelled against their moral philosophy, have at any rate managed to convey a personal attitude of great moral concern, and a willingness to write in the spirit of the age. In a Christian setting, this more existentialist approach has often been expressed in terms of the commandment to love and of the personal guidance of the Holy Spirit in the uniqueness of each moral situation. It is my own view that a mood of moral concern is but a poor substitute for the painstaking analysis of moral issues, and that much recent writing on Christian ethics has suffered from many philosophical defects and from a pervasive vagueness which makes it of little real use. Several of the key terms are left all too often completely undefined, such as 'love' or 'conscience', 'unique' or 'universal'; moral evaluation of agents is confused with moral evaluation of actions or of states of affairs; conclusions are held to follow from premises which would equally justify other incompatible conclusions; and so on. There is, I think, enough criticism of such theories in recent philosophical writing for me not to have to repeat it here.[1]

[1] See Frankena (2), Harrison, ch.8, and Macquarrie, ch.2.

On the other hand, it must be said that many recent presentations of natural law theory have richly deserved the criticisms levelled against them. There is more than the suspicion that 'natural law' arguments have been manipulated in order to produce predetermined conclusions. If the radicals have failed to define 'love', for example, so natural law theorists have failed to give adequate accounts of such key notions as 'function' or even 'nature' itself. Again, natural law theory has frequently suffered from an overemphasis on those aspects of human nature which are most easily studied, and has thus stressed arguments based on biology and physiology at the expense of arguments based on, say, sociology or psychology. Most unfortunately, the use of the term 'the natural law' has given the impression that only one theory of this type has ever been advanced. The result has been that it has become more and more divorced from contemporary moral philosophy, an impoverishment which natural law theories can least of all afford. A further consequence has been that it has been easy for critics of one particular version of natural law theory to reject the whole approach. Much recent natural law theory, in my opinion, has contributed to its own decline in Christian circles, and, more seriously, to the popularity of the various philosophically incoherent theories launched under the banner of 'situation ethics'. The radical critic needs to be convinced that the natural law approach to ethics can indeed deal with the interpersonal, social and political problems in a constructive and realistic way.

To say to the radical critic that there are other versions of natural law theory which he might care to consider as well as the one he has rejected is, however, to play rather into the hands of his conservative counterpart. The conservative points to the wide range of disagreement among moral philosophers as evidence of the uncertainty and unreliability of the discipline in contrast to the clarity of an ethic based on revelation. I have already given my reasons for disputing the second part of this position; but I think many moral theologians might well sympathize with the view that if Christian ethics is handed over to moral philosophers nobody will know where they are any longer. I have already alluded to the difficulties allegedly encountered in producing natural law arguments against divorce and remarriage, and to the widely held view that there will too rarely be any solution to pressing moral problems unless appeal is made to, say, texts of the New Testament. I think that a similar fear underlies the tendency to insist on what are termed 'authentic interpretations' of the natural law by some Catholic theologians.

To difficulties urged along these lines there is no very simple solution, any more than there is an easy answer to the radical critic. It must be admitted that the study of human nature, and the attempt to interpret human nature in moral terms, is a difficult enterprise, ill-calculated to produce neat and easy solutions to our moral dilemmas. What I think needs to be challenged is the implicit conservative assumption that unless we can assure ourselves that we have all the correct answers, we will inevitably be tormented by doubt, paralysed by insecurity, or divided by our disagreements. Aquinas, for example, pointed out that the more detailed the problem one tries to tackle, the less clear we will normally be able to be about how natural law applies to it; but he seems to have been able to say this without any great qualms.[2] And I take it to be part and parcel of normal adult human life that serious decisions often enough have to be taken without our having all the information on which such a decision should ideally be based. Lack of total moral clarity is indeed a challenge which is at times painful; but I see no reason to suppose that God somehow wishes to rescue us from having to face it.

The conservative criticism is to this extent just, however, in that unless the natural law approach can produce as much guidance as can reasonably be expected, and unless it can point at least the direction in which moral progress lies, then it will fail as a moral theory. The task of this chapter, then, is to produce a theory of ethics which at least gives promise of being able to deal with contemporary problems in a way which might satisfy the radical critic, and which is sufficiently precise to meet any reasonable demand for clarity and guidance. In a work of this scope, it is manifestly impossible to work out such a theory in all its implications, and I will make no pretence at completeness. In particular, I shall devote comparatively little space to consideration of the theory of justice.[3]

---

[2] S.T. I–II, 94.4.   [3] For the complexities, see Rawls, Daniels, and Miller.

I shall attempt no more than an outline of the basic elements which, in my view, an adequate moral theory must contain. I shall be more than content if it turns out to have started in the right way, and offers some promise that it could be developed satisfactorily along the lines I shall indicate.

Basic Pre-Moral Facts

A natural law theory takes its origin from our knowledge of man as he is. It must therefore begin by asking what we do in fact know about man, and how this knowledge is arrived at. The answer is surprisingly complex. Much of our knowledge is informal in character, gained almost imperceptibly through the mere process of living in human society. It would be almost impossible to itemize the things we have learnt about human beings just by the experiences of our friends and by a hundred and one other ways which almost defy description and analysis. To take some examples quite at random; I have some knowledge of the difference between Frenchmen, Spaniards, Englishmen and Germans; some appreciation of the different social structure in a suburb of Glasgow and a suburb of London; a good idea of the behaviour to expect of a crowd at a football match, a cocktail party, a funeral or a philosophy seminar; comedians know how to make audiences laugh, mothers know when their children are sickening for something, politicians know just how much pressure someone can stand.

More formally, we have gained a great deal of knowledge of man in his environment through the development of the various scientific disciplines. Without attempting anything like a complete list, one might mention firstly the directly human sciences, such as medicine, psychology, sociology, economics, history and geography; and, more indirectly, we would have to include physics, chemistry, biochemistry, genetics, engineering, meteorology and soil-analysis, all of which provide knowledge which can have an immediate bearing on the environment in which we have to live and function. Not all of these sciences are equally advanced, and some of them are still in their infancy. It might be argued that the social sciences should not be expected to develop along the lines pioneered by the physical sciences, and that their method and approach should be peculiarly their own. But be that as it may, each of these disciplines must develop criteria of rigour and self-criticism; and to the extent that they succeed in this, the results that they produce will be worthy of our belief and, ideally, will count as knowledge gained. Our knowledge of man, then, is a combination of informal knowledge gained from our experience of life, and more systematic knowledge to the extent that it has been made available to us by the advance of the sciences.

I do not wish to claim that any of this knowledge is moral knowledge. But (if I may anticipate the subsequent discussion for a moment) it seems to me to be beyond argument that knowledge of this kind is an indispensable condition for any moral knowledge we might attain. To put the point somewhat differently, if any natural law theory depends on our knowledge of what man is like, then it will be impossible in such a theory to know more about morality than can be supported by the current state of our informal and scientific knowledge generally. Of course we are perfectly capable of acting on the basis of the best available opinion, as we frequently must. But we should be extremely chary of claims which seek to transmute respectable moral claims, based on respectable non-moral beliefs (whether informal or scientific), into instances of moral knowledge. Moral theory does not exist in some change-less quasi-Platonic universe, unaffected by the state of the relevant sciences or the extent of our non-moral experience.

The assertions of the previous paragraph will have to be argued for later. Something must be said at this point to forestall the philosophical objection that *any* view is untenable which proposes to connect moral knowledge with non-moral knowledge in the way I have implied. I am not arguing for just *any* connection, let it be said. I am not, for example, willing to content myself with a purely psychological connection, such as that someone holding particular non-moral beliefs would also tend to approve of certain courses of action and would be unlikely to favour certain others. Nor am I willing to be satisfied with the view that although anyone making a moral decision will give an account of that decision in terms of non-moral beliefs which he has, there is no logical connection between those beliefs and the moral principle underlying his decision. Although, as will be made clear, I am not willing to accept the term without qualification, for the moment it is simplest to say that I shall be arguing in favour of a theory which is (partly, at least) a naturalist one. (It is as well to be clear that not all naturalist theories are natural law theories: views which define moral duty in terms of the will of God would for the most part count as naturalist theories in the philosophical sense.)

It is still widely held that G.E. Moore long ago made any naturalist theory untenable, and that he did so by showing that there was some kind of logical fallacy involved in giving an account of the meaning of moral terms by means of terms which were non-moral.[4] I do not intend to rehearse here all the arguments which might be adduced against Moore.[5] Suffice it to say that he was plainly mistaken in supposing (if he did suppose this) that there is any *fallacy* involved in defining moral words in terms of non-moral words. The anti-naturalist arguments in Moore and in his later followers succeed in doing no more than beg the question. They assume without much proof that there is a clear distinction to be drawn between the objects of moral knowledge and the objects of other kinds of knowledge; or they assume that there is a sharp distinction to be drawn between describing and commending, or between facts and values. To be sure, in saying that these objections simply beg the question I am not thereby showing them to be mistaken. I am saying no more than that the issue must be settled on other and wider grounds. It seems to me that the main areas of controversy between naturalists and their critics are two: firstly, how exactly we are to distinguish the moral from the non-moral quite generally; and secondly, whether it is possible without circularity to determine which non-moral truths are relevant evidence in support of moral assertions.

Despite his rejection of naturalism in ethics, however, Moore would have agreed with me in speaking, as I have done, of moral knowledge, and in saying that to describe something as good, or an action as obligatory, was genuinely to give a description of it (although this description was, in Moore's view, a description of a

---

[4] This I take to be the best way of reading Moore's rather unclear point.
[5] See Frankena (1) and Nakhnikian.

unique and somewhat peculiar kind). In contrast to this cognitivist account of moral utterances is a current popular tendency to dismiss such utterances, along with aesthetic utterances, as 'mere value judgments' or as contrasted with statements of fact as being 'up to the individual to decide'. This popular view is largely the result of a confusion, I think, related to the mistaken view that to set out to establish criteria for moral truth is to set out to be morally intolerant towards others. However, there is a more philosophical argument to the effect that it is mistaken to look for truth, in the proper sense of the word, in moral judgments as such (although it may well be that such judgments presuppose other, non-moral, beliefs which *can* be true or false). There is much to be said in favour of Stevenson's emotivist account of the force of moral utterances to which I shall return later,[6] and much to be said for Hare's insistence that logic alone cannot suffice to settle substantive moral disputes, of which more presently. However, Stevenson and Hare have too rapidly concluded that Moore conclusively demonstrated that the object of moral knowledge could not be identical with the object of any other kind of knowledge (although the moral point of view might well be different from the standpoint of other sciences). Still, in so doing they insist on two points which I believe to be correct, and which will serve as a useful introduction to my own discussion.

Hare is quite correct, it seems to me, in his contention that *merely* to offer a substantive definition of a moral word such as 'good' in terms of some non-moral word such as, say, 'pleasure', and thus to take the first step in relating morality to non-moral fact, will fail to settle any dispute about ethics. Someone who disagrees with the resulting conclusions will simply refuse to accept the proffered definitions, and there is no logical means to compel him to reconsider the matter. Thus, I have myself already argued against any definitional equivalence between 'duty' and 'what God wills'. Definitions are not the kind of thing that can be true or false, and one cannot in the strict sense make a mistake about a definition unless one intends a definition to be no more than a

---

[6] Stevenson, esp. chapters 1–5, and the invaluable discussion in Urmson.

report of how the word is in fact used. Equally, the propriety of a definition cannot be proved by logic, any more than it can be simply on the basis of common usage. Wider considerations have to be invoked. Thus, I argued against defining 'duty' as 'what God wills' because adopting such a definition has unacceptable consequences for the Christian picture of God. It follows, I believe, that definitions in general will be acceptable only if it can be shown that the consequences of adopting them will be so desirable that the cost of rejecting them would be unacceptably high. This will not be the case if the proposed definition is perceived as begging all the important moral questions right from the outset.

The second point on which Hare and Stevenson are quite correct, as it seems to me, is their rejection of Moore's intuitionist account of the way we justify our assertions of moral value. That is to say, they reject the view that moral truths can be said simply to be known without any further argument or evidence being adduced. (Hare and Stevenson would, of course, in addition wish to qualify or deny Moore's view that moral utterances can be genuine *statements*.) I would not myself wish to argue that there can be *no* instances of knowledge which need no further justification; I do not see anything irreducibly problematic about the notion of self-warranting knowledge. As it seems to me, the basic argument against most intuitionist theories of ethics is that intuition is appealed to in a way which makes the theory as a whole powerless. One of the functions which a moral theory ought to be able to perform is the resolution of moral disagreements. As a matter of fact, we have very many moral disagreements, both about general principles, and about their application to particular situations. To appeal to intuition at this point is fruitless – all that is needed is for the other party to the disagreement to claim a counter-intuition and the argument can proceed no further. If claims to intuition are going to be made, it is essential, I think, that those claims cannot sensibly be called in question. Now it is in principle possible, I suppose, to hold that the ultimate statements in an ethical theory are known intuitively to be true, provided that these statements are not open to serious challenge. In practice, I think that it is almost impossible to produce a set of ultimate ethical principles for which such a claim could be made.

I propose, therefore, to try another approach which, I hope, will meet both the criticisms anti-naturalists offer of the definition of moral terms, and which will also avoid the objections to intuitionist ethics. In so doing, however, I hope to establish at least one crucial element in the naturalist position, by relating the basic pre-moral facts to specifically moral judgments within the scope of the theory as a whole.

The Nature of a Moral Theory

The functions which we should like a moral theory to perform are fairly obvious. We should like a moral theory to support the moral judgments we make, and to enable us to decide between true and false moral beliefs. We should also like it to enable us to deal with situations which we have not previously encountered, so that we could say what ought to be done in them, and give good reasons for so saying. To this extent a moral theory is expected to perform at least the same kinds of functions as a scientific theory, and I wish to pursue this analogy rather further.

I take it that the main features of a scientific theory are roughly as follows. The starting point is a set of data — perhaps informal observations in the first instance, but in the end a series of measurements which can be made rather more accurately. The data are chosen in the first instance because they are connected with phenomena which interest us; but it is also true that at a somewhat later stage the theory itself to some extent predetermines the data which it undertakes to interpret. Thus, it may be that to begin with we wish to discover why all the patients in a particular ward of a hospital became ill with stomach pains on the same day. We start off by observing that they are all ill; more precisely, we can take their temperatures and blood-pressures and so forth. It may turn out that we can find one simple explanation which covers all the cases. But it may also turn out that we can find one explanation to cover all but, say, two of the cases, and no one explanation to cover them all. Depending on other features of the situation we may in the end decide either that our explanation is unsatisfactory because it did not deal with all the data, or we might decide to accept the theory as adequate for those cases which it covers, and seek some other explanation for the other two. We might discover, for instance, that there was a perfectly straightforward explanation for them, too; on the other hand we might find out that the tests run on the two patients had been improperly conducted, and that the evidence we initially began with — temperatures, cultures, blood-counts, or whatever — was itself misleading. In short, data and theory-production to some extent interact. Theories can ignore data which was originally thought relevant, or can lead us to question data we originally took for granted; or the theory can simply account for all the data we started with.

The theory itself will consist of an interrelated set of definitions, assumptions, and rules enabling us to derive conclusions from previous statements of certain kinds. An acceptable theory will have several characteristics; its assumptions will be comparatively few and comparatively simple; it will not generate contradictory solutions; it will successfully deal with new situations as well as with the data with which it started. It will not be claimed that its basic assumptions are self-evident or that they are known by intuition, but simply that on the basis of these assumptions a satisfactory theory can be built. Its definitions and rules of inference will be justified in the same way. True statements will then be just those that can be justified within the theory.

This much is, I believe, reasonably uncontroversial as an account of scientific theories. Its application to ethics is less obvious. What, for example, are the data which it is the function of an ethical theory to explain? What will count as a successful explanation in ethics, as distinct from an unsuccessful one? Which are the primitive assumptions which are to be made?

I think it is worth pursuing the idea that the data which it is the purpose of an ethical theory to explain are the moral beliefs which people in fact have, or have had. The type of explanation in which we are interested is not the kind of explanation which might be offered by a psychologist, or a sociologist, or a historian. In these cases, what would be explained would be the formation of the beliefs, and the explanation would doubtless be in terms of parental influence, the economic situation, the influence of other cultures, and so forth. I take it that the task of an ethical theory is to exhibit the multiplicity of ethical beliefs that people have in terms of a simple set of basic assumptions, definitions, rules of inference and patterns of argument, in terms of which these beliefs might be justified. As in the case of any theory, some of the initial data might in the end be ignored, or rejected as misleading. I do not imagine that a successful ethical theory will have to provide a justification for all the ethical beliefs that men have. For one thing, it may well be that men hold incompatible ethical beliefs, and there will be no merit in a theory which results in our saying that incompatible assertions are equally true within the theory. On the other hand, it will not do to produce a theory which is unable to deal with a large proportion of its initial data. An ethical theory which exhibited as false a large number of the ethical beliefs people held as true would simply fail as an adequate theory. Moreover, just as it is an advantage, in the case of a scientific theory, if we can explain how the misleading data arose in the first place — say, by discovering a faulty instrument or some external interference with an experiment — so, too, it seems to me that in the case of ethics it will be an advantage if there is an independent explanation to be found for moral beliefs which the theory rejects as false. Such an explanation might consist, for instance, in a mistaken factual premiss being used in the argument, or in failure to identify correctly the action being evaluated.

I propose, then, to regard the basic assumptions of an ethical theory in the same way as one might regard Newton's Laws or the axioms of a geometric system; not as truths which are either self-evident or intuited, but as assumptions which in the end are justified by their simplicity, consistency, and, in the long run, by the satisfactory way in which the system to which they give rise can explain the data in which we are interested. Definitions are to be regarded in a similar light. If the theory as a whole works, the basic assumptions and definitions can be challenged only at the cost of losing the explanatory power of the theory, which will be too high a cost to pay.

I shall take it as axiomatic that our morality will depend, somehow or other, on the kind of beings that human beings are. This might appear to be an unwise first move, open right at the beginning to a Kantian challenge: ought not morality to depend solely on those features which all moral agents have in common?[7] Would the Christian not also wish to speak of God in moral terms, for example? But I think that these objections will not in fact be pressed very hard. In the case of God, it is of course true that Christians will use moral terms of God, and that part of recognizing that God *is* God involves recognizing that he is morally good. But the description of God in moral terms must involve the analogous use of those terms, and the analogy must in the first instance be drawn from our experience of human morality. It may be that what it is to be moral for God is quite other than for us; but all that we can *say* about God's morality will have to be said in ways which are meaningful in human terms. Nor will the Kantian wish to press the point very hard. I believe that Kant's remark about morality applying to all rational agents as such has to do with the form of morality, and in particular with praiseworthiness and blameworthiness, and does not at all exclude the necessity for, say, moral Martians to behave in a different way from moral human beings. Even Kant is perfectly willing to introduce 'anthropology' in giving *content* to the moral law. Moreover, I am not even as confident as Kant that it makes sense to speak of the form of morality being the same for all rational agents, as if we could rely on the univocity of the term 'rational'. It may be just as covertly anthropomorphic to ask about Martian moral thinking as it is to ask whether certain insects ought to eat the male with whom they have just mated (or, for that matter, to ask whether God ought to have created the world as he did). At any rate, since I intend my remarks to apply only to morality for human beings, it seems to me that I need have no dispute with Kant if I assume that that morality will in some manner depend on the kind of being we are.

The Area of the Moral

There are four areas in which we use evaluative language which are distinct, and whose interrelationships must be clarified before we try to delimit the area of the moral. These areas may be listed as follows:

[7] Kant, § § 410–412.

(1) We describe persons in their behaviour as praiseworthy, blameworthy, negligent, of diminished responsibility, and so on.

(2) We evaluate characters and traits of character as mature, disreputable, possessive, spiteful, trustworthy, honest, etc.

(3) We describe objects, states of affairs, activities and events as good, undesirable, unfortunate, unjust, etc.

(4) We also use these words to describe particular pieces of human behaviour. In using the neutral term 'pieces of behaviour' in 4, I have deliberately avoided the much more difficult term 'action'. Thus, the kind of example I have in mind as an instance of 4 could be illustrated by such remarks as 'What he is doing is simply wrong' or 'Her behaviour yesterday was really outrageous' or 'That was very kind of you'. It seems fairly clear that evaluations of this type are always dependent on some other type of evaluation. A piece of behaviour will be evaluated either in terms of its consequences or in terms of the kind of activity which it constituted. Thus, if I ask why what he did was wrong, the answer is either going to be of the form, 'Because it caused his wife needless pain' or of the form 'Because it was stealing'. In short, evaluations of type-4 will always depend ultimately on some evaluation of type-3.

Evaluations of character and character-traits of type-2 are similarly dependent on evaluations of the kind of behaviour in which characters of that sort typically engage, or on the kinds of activity which can be expected of them. Of course it is true that people can act out of character, and there is no logical connection between having a particular character or trait and always acting in a certain way. Nevertheless, I think we consider someone disreputable only if in general he can be expected to behave disreputably. Once again, evaluations of type-3 turn out to be more fundamental than those of type-2.

Evaluations of type-1 are more complex. Often enough, we will base our estimates of persons in their behaviour on our antecedent knowledge of their character. If someone is in general known to be kind, he may well be given the benefit of the doubt if we see him doing something as a result of which other people suffer; and if someone is in general known to be grasping and dishonest, we will view even apparently innocent activities of his with a good deal of suspicion. On the other hand, we know that people can act out of character, and it is therefore not the case that evaluations of type-1 depend simply or even necessarily on type-2 estimates of their characters. It would more often be the case that we evaluate persons in their behaviour on the basis of our estimates of that behaviour itself. In general, persons are blameworthy if what they do is wrong, or spiteful, or whatever, and praiseworthy if what they do is good. But, of course, even this connection can be overridden in individual cases. Someone who does something wrong may have an excuse which makes it illegitimate to blame him; and someone who does something which has good results may simply have been lucky, or may have done it for disreputable motives, in which case we will not give him much credit for it. Thus, although type-4 evaluations of people's behaviour provide the background against which type-1 questions about praise, blame, and moral credit arise, many further complicating factors are involved in estimating persons in their behaviour. Type-1 evaluations are not simply reducible to those of type-4, and hence are not simply reducible to those of type-3.

In short, it appears that the fundamental types of evaluation are those of objects, states of affairs, activities and events, on the one hand, and on the other of persons in their behaviour. Estimates of character and of particular pieces of behaviour can be reduced to these two, but they cannot be reduced one to the other. We are now in a position to inquire whether and in what circumstances evaluations of persons in their behaviour (type-1) and estimates of objects, events, activities and states of affairs (type-3) are properly moral evaluations.

It is Kant's view, I think, that only type-1 evaluations of persons in their behaviour are properly to be considered as moral evaluations, although these properly moral evaluations will depend on non-moral characteristics of the actions or activities in which those persons engage. I take it that when Kant says that only the good will can be said to be good in an absolute sense, he means by 'absolute' what I would mean by 'moral'; hence he goes on to say that riches, or health, or other good states of affairs are indeed good, but cannot be said to be good in the full sense (i.e. morally good).[8] And if we take a piece of behaviour (type-4), Kant would

[8]   Kant, § § 393–4.

say, as I have said, that evaluation of the piece of behaviour can be made only in terms of the maxim, the subjective description of that behaviour, which the agent proposes to himself; that is to say, Kant holds that behaviour can be evaluated only in terms of activities, or states of affairs, or consequences (since it is these features which will appear in the maxim). We cannot evaluate simply 'what he is doing'; we must evaluate it under some description, such as 'wasting his talents' or 'breaking a promise' or 'committing adultery'. Moreover; in Kant's view, the relevant description is the one *which the agent gives himself* as an account of his action. Thus it may be that an observer would describe what John is doing as breaking a promise; but John (who has forgotten he promised to meet a friend) might describe his own action as 'spending a nasty wet evening comfortably by the fire with a good book'. Whether this action is a violation of duty or not depends, for Kant, on a non-moral feature of the action, namely, whether or not it is possible to will that its maxim should serve as a universal law. There is some doubt about exactly what this test involves, but it seems to me clear at least that it is meant to involve some kind of consistency, and consistency is a non-moral matter. Thus, Kant's view can be summed up, I submit, as follows: the only fully moral evaluation is the evaluation involved in saying, for example, that John was quite blameless in spending the evening at home as he did; and to say that the action of spending the evening at home violated no duty is to say something about the consistency with which John was able to will that action. That Kant is willing to use terms like 'duty' or 'obligation' in connection with actions and activities suggests that, at least in a wider sense, he is willing to regard these as *moral* evaluations; but I think he is willing to do this only because of the close connection between such actions and the fully moral evaluation of John in his performance of them.

In all this, I believe Kant to be quite correct in his insistence that the primary interest of our moral evaluations is in persons in their behaviour. I suggest that much of the contemporary unwillingness to make moral judgments about actions, expressed in such slogans as 'I can't make moral judgments about what other people do, that's up to their consciences' reflects, albeit in a confused way, this basic Kantian point.

It seems to me that little more than terminology is at stake when we ask whether or not we should describe as 'moral' the evaluations we make of actions or activities (pieces of behaviour under a certain description). I propose that we should agree that these evaluations are moral, although in a different, and possibly wider, sense of 'moral' than that involved in speaking of someone as morally blameworthy. To this extent, I think I am following Kant. Where I propose to depart from him is in being willing to evaluate certain states of affairs in this wider 'moral' sense. Thus it seems to me that when I describe the position of the blacks in South Africa as unjust, this is a moral evaluation of that position. The departure from Kant is not very great, however, for even here I am considering the situation as one which has been produced by human actions; I could not describe the misery and deprivation resulting from an earthquake or a cyclone as a situation of injustice.

Consider now other evaluations of objects, activities, and states of affairs. I think that money is a good thing, and that sailing, or hill-walking, or praying are good kinds of activity, and that to be starving or deprived or in pain are bad states to be in. Kant is surely right in saying that these evaluations are not in themselves moral evaluations at all. Still, it is surely also true that these evaluations will often be highly relevant to moral evaluations, whether in the wider or the stricter sense. The reason for this is not far to seek. Reference to such objects, activities, or states of affairs will turn up in the descriptions of actions which are the object of moral evaluation in the wider sense, and these actions will to some extent underlie our evaluations of persons performing them which are moral in the narrowest sense.

I therefore propose the following schema:

- *Moral evaluations in the strict sense* are evaluations of persons in their behaviour, as deserving of praise or blame.
- *Moral evaluations in the wider sense* are evaluations of actions (where 'action' is to be taken, roughly, as an intentional piece of behaviour under a certain description).
- *Morally relevant evaluations* are those evaluations of objects, activities, or states of affairs which underlie the wider and stricter kind of moral evaluations.

In this book I shall have nothing further to say about moral evaluations in the strict sense, nor about the theory of excuses with which they are intimately connected. Instead, I shall concentrate on moral evaluations in the wider sense, and on trying to determine which other kinds of evaluation are properly to be considered as morally relevant.

We have at least a rough understanding of which decisions raise moral issues and which do not, a distinction which it is one of the tasks of a moral theory to explain. We would not normally consider any of the following situations to involve a moral decision:

> Whether or not to move Q–R5 in a chess game
> Which shoe to put on first
> Which colour to paint the kitchen
> What to have for dinner

Although these decisions are not normally of any moral significance, it is worth asking whether we can imagine circumstances in which they might be. Suppose, for example, I am playing chess with an old man whose one remaining pleasure it is, and who feels that it is the one thing he can still do well; and suppose that Q–R5 is a move which would turn the tables on him completely and enable me to win against all the run of the play. I might now wonder whether or not to make the move, and whether it might not be better to make some other move simply as a kindness to him. And I might then wonder whether such kindness might not in the end be patronizing, or, if he spotted it, self-defeating; I might ask myself whether he would be made miserable by losing to a player of my (normally) poor standard, and so on. At this point, it seems to me, I would be thinking of the decision in moral terms. Again, I might conceivably have some peculiar spinal weakness such that to bend down to the left without previously having bent down to the right was liable to incapacitate me for hours or even days. In such circumstances, I might consider it irresponsible to put on my left shoe first, because of the trouble it might cause me and my family or friends. It seems to me that 'irresponsible' here has moral overtones. And, without being so far-fetched, we can easily see how to paint the kitchen a colour which one's wife is known to hate, or to serve a meal which the guests (for reasons, say, of health or of religion) are unable to eat, would plainly be morally wrong. Such examples could easily be multiplied. What they show, I believe, is that actions are seen as morally significant just when we can see that they have some connection with human welfare. I think that this conclusion is quite generally applicable. The criterion for distinguishing between the morally significant and the morally non-significant is the presence or absence of a connection with human welfare.[9]

This conclusion at first sight might seem to be both too narrow and too wide. Too narrow, in that it says nothing about the welfare of animals, and too wide in that it will result in our having to describe as morally significant actions or features of actions which we should not normally describe in that way.

I am inclined to think that what I have said ought to be broadened to include animals to the extent that we can see parallels between the welfare of animals and that of human beings. But I have no very satisfactory way of drawing the line here. It would not be too outlandish to suggest that it is, for example, morally wrong to maltreat horses or dogs or cows; and we can at least understand the moral concern shown by people who disapprove of battery-chicken farming. On the other hand, we kill greenfly without compunction, simply because they may deprive us of the pleasure of looking at our roses, which would be hard to justify did we think that the welfare of greenfly was morally significant; it is not even as if they spread infection as some other insects do. So, while I would be sympathetic to the suggestion that my criterion ought somehow to be broadened in this general direction, I am far from clear about how this is to be done.[10]

In the other direction, the criterion might seem somewhat too broad, since it would suggest that decisions about where to go on holiday, what car (if any) to buy, what job to take, and whom to marry, would all turn out to be morally significant decisions, and the problems in taking them would turn out to be moral problems, since all of them have a fairly obvious connection with human welfare. I suspect that it would not occur to most people most of the

---

[9] Wallace and Walker is a useful collection of other views.

[10] Clark's full-length study of this problem has just come to my attention. I have not been able to take account of his discussion, but a full-length treatment of the subject is surely long overdue.

time to see these as moral decisions, though they might see them as important in other ways. Still, I am inclined to say that our ordinary usage may well be misleading here. We can anyway point to quite uncontroversial instances of our usage of 'moral' being too narrow: 'Doctor arrested on morals charge' is clear enough, and idiomatic enough, but should not, I suggest, be allowed to count as evidence for the scope of the word 'moral'. The situation perhaps is that we tend to use 'immoral' only for the most important or flagrant kinds of immorality, and that other words like 'wrong' will more naturally be used, still in a clearly moral sense, for less striking cases. In any event, the counter-evidence to my proposal does not strike me as strong enough to outweigh the fact that the kinds of considerations which we adduce in order to show that something is after all a moral issue are considerations to do with human welfare.

It may well be a consequence of this view that most, perhaps even all, pieces of human behaviour will turn out to have moral significance. However, not all descriptions of this behaviour will include a reference to those features of the behaviour in virtue of which it is morally significant; 'painting the kitchen blue' or 'scoring a try' or 'walking down the street' are actions which, so described, are not morally significant, although the behaviour involved may well have been.

All in all, then, I think it is a fair working hypothesis that all and only those features of human behaviour are morally relevant which have a bearing on human welfare (with some possible qualification to include animals). It follows from this that all such features are relevant when we come to assess our behaviour, and that no other features are relevant. The same point can also be made with regard to objects, events, and states of affairs.

It is a conceptual truth that human welfare depends somehow or other, in a way which I shall attempt to clarify in the next section, upon the satisfaction of human desires. It need not, indeed, be the case that welfare requires the satisfaction of all the desires we have. But it does not make sense to speak of someone's welfare as being ensured if none of their desires are satisfied; that a desire is satisfied is *prima facie* evidence that some contribution has been made to a person's welfare, and that a desire is frustrated is *prima facie* evidence that someone's welfare is to that extent impeded. If we combine this with the view that the difference between the morally significant and the morally non-significant is connected with human welfare, we may conclude that a favourable moral evaluation will be connected somehow with the satisfaction of desires, and an unfavourable moral evaluation with their frustration.

I hope to have shown by this argument that there is a conceptual connection between moral evaluation and the satisfaction of human desires, and to that extent to have laid the foundation for what is a (partially) naturalist theory of ethics. I propose this result not as something which is self-evidently true, nor as a purely reportive definition of 'moral evaluation', but as a hypothesis on the basis of which our moral beliefs can be explained. I think the cost of rejecting this hypothesis is that it will not be possible otherwise to account for the way in which we draw the distinction between morally significant and non-significant features of actions, events, or states of affairs. On the other hand, it is clear that this account is quite inadequate as it stands, and that it will do only if a much more careful look is taken at the way in which desires are to be satisfied. This will be the object of the next section.

Needs, Wants and Urges

The attempt to base a moral theory on an account of human desires has several difficulties to overcome. Given the strange desires that some people have, it might well seem as if any theory based on desires will lead to far too many intolerable conclusions for it to count as a satisfactory explanation of the moral beliefs which people actually have. No theory can afford to reject too large a proportion of its data as misleading or unreliable. To base the theory upon needs rather than desires might seem a much more promising move; it is less implausible to suggest that we have a duty to satisfy people's needs than to suggest that we satisfy their desires. It would therefore be helpful to be able to exclude some desires as not representing genuine needs. But we cannot simply beg the question by ruling 'undesirable' desires out of court right from the start. To do so would be to introduce too many assumptions which have not been argued for, and which would doubtless prove too controversial for it to be possible simply to stipulate that they are basic assumptions.

Moreover, it might be argued that people's needs, let alone their desires, are so varied that any theory based on them will inevitably turn out to be relativist, and that this is an unfortunate conclusion to reach. At the end of Chapter IV I shall argue that the charge of relativism is by no means clear, and that considerable argument must take place before it can be decided what relativism involves, and whether a theory is relativist or not. I shall, however, endeavour to prove that an account of ethics based on human needs need not be relativist in any damaging sense.

Ideally, the advantage to be gained from a moral theory based on needs is that it then becomes comparatively clear how one is to check the results of it. It offers a procedure by which one can set about deciding what ought and what ought not to be done. Bentham was, it seems to me, entirely right in his contention that moral convictions (especially those based on an intuitionist view of ethics) tend to be no better than 'what in others we would term prejudice' unless they can be tested by a procedure which is both clear and readily available. But if this is to work, we must devise a method of identifying needs from among the host of desires that we have; and in addition we must, I think, be in a position to know when a desire has or has not been satisfied. The remainder of this section will be devoted to developing a critique of desires which embodies no morally controversial assumptions and yet will yield a list of needs which can be used to explain our moral beliefs in a satisfactory manner. I hope it will both exhibit at least our central and most important beliefs about ethics as justified; and I hope that it will provide a procedure for resolving new moral dilemmas which we have not had to face before and about which we have as yet no clear beliefs. But first it is necessary to look for a moment at our knowledge of our desires.

We express some of our desires in terms of wants. I wish to use both 'desire' and 'want' in such a way as to cover both inclinations we have, and policies we have adopted. Thus, in the first sense, it may be true that I want simply to get out of this room and away from all these boring people; yet in the second sense I might want to stay, because there is someone I have said I would meet here. I think it is true of all those desires which we could express as wants that we know whether or not that desire has been satisfied. If I say that I have got what I wanted, it does not make sense, as I am using the term, for someone else to query whether this is in fact true. To be sure, someone might query whether I truly needed what I said I wanted, and whether in some other sense I might not still remain unsatisfied even when I have got what I said I wanted. But this is different from my not having got what I said I wanted.

The situation is rather more complicated with unconscious desires. I do not wish to exclude all talk of such desires, for to postulate the existence of unconscious desires may well be the best way of explaining otherwise puzzling features of our actual behaviour. I suppose that there may be some cases of unconscious desires in which we are not consciously aware of any dissatisfaction at all, and where the existence of such desires could be established only by expert analysis of my behaviour. I think it will have to be admitted that in the case of these desires I myself will not necessarily be in a position to say whether or not they have been satisfied. All that I can say about these is firstly, that they are certainly relevant to ethics; and secondly, that our knowledge in this area will be indirect, and will depend on the relevant psychological theory. On the other hand, it may well be the case that we have some desires which are conscious sources of dissatisfaction, but which we are unable to formulate clearly as wants, or which we formulate as wants which a psychiatrist, for example, would take to be symbolic representations of the desire in question rather than as adequate expressions of that desire. In these cases, I think it is true to say that I myself am incorrigible when I claim that the desire is, or is not, satisfied.

In short, I will take it that in so far as desires are consciously present to us, and whether or not we can adequately express them in terms of wants, we know whether or not those desires are satisfied.

Now let us consider needs. I shall use the term 'need' in such a way that it is a necessary truth that human welfare consists in the satisfaction of all a person's needs. What evidence do we have to help us in identifying what these needs are? It seems to me that the evidence must consist in the existence of a desire. I can see no other way in which we would ever conclude that we had a need for something, if that need did not turn up somewhere or other as a desire. As I remarked above, it may not be the case that the desire is consciously present to us, and the evidence for a need may therefore be indirect. In the rest of this section, however, I shall not be concerned with evidence of this kind. I shall be dealing simply with those needs which we are aware of because we are aware of the existence of desires. We can try, sometimes successfully, and sometimes unsuccessfully, to express our desires in terms of wants. With the partial exception of wholly unconscious desires, then, the evidence that we have a need is to be found in the things that we say we want. Plainly this evidence will need to be scrutinized carefully. We know that many of our wants are capricious, impulsive and misguided; and if the mere existence of a want were to be conclusive evidence of the existence of a corresponding need connected with human welfare, we would be faced with the unpalatable conclusion that our welfare involved being spiteful, capricious, selfish and even neurotic; for many of our wants exhibit just those characteristics.

What is required, then, is a theory which will succeed in filtering out from among all the things people say they want those wants which are evidence of needs. I am going to suggest four elements which such a filtering mechanism must contain and which a want must pass through if it is to count as an expression of a need. It will be my contention that the construction of these filters will beg no important moral question, but that, taken together, these filters will enable us to take an effective first step in the resolution of moral questions.

Wants based on false beliefs

The beliefs to which I shall be referring in this section are non-moral beliefs, such as those which are to be found in the scientific disciplines mentioned at the start of this chapter, together with the mass of informal beliefs that we have, such as that there is a chair in the room, or that John loves Mary, or that trains for Glasgow leave from Euston, or that the pound notes handed to me as change in the shop are genuine. Some of these beliefs, both the scientific and the informal ones, are false; but we are in general equipped with means for determining which are false and which are true, and it is important that these means have nothing to do with morals as such.

Whenever we say that we want something, it is necessarily also true that we have certain beliefs about it. We must be able to identify it just in order to express the want; and identification cannot take place without some beliefs being held. In addition, we must, I think, believe that what it is that we want will satisfy some desire, or else it would not be a *want* that we were expressing. Both sets of beliefs may be false in a given case. Now, it may be that we want something only because we have some false belief(s) about it. Did we not hold this false belief, we would not have that want at all. Thus I may want a picture only because I have falsely identified it as a Rembrandt; and I may want a ladder only because I falsely believe it will be long enough to enable me to reach the windows I wish to wash. Wants can range over particular things, like that picture, that ladder, or to send my son to Eton, as well as over types of thing, such as to go to university, or get a well-paid job, or simply to get away from it all. The test for whether a want is based on a false belief is whether the person still wants what he previously wanted once his false beliefs about it have been corrected.

Some uncontroversial examples may illustrate the point. John may have a headache which he wants to get rid of. Seeing two tablets on the table, and believing them to be aspirin, he may then say that he wants the tablets on the table over there. Suppose that John is then informed that the tablets are not aspirin but penicillin. John will usually no longer want to take them. Again, Bert may wish to marry Angela, because he believes that they can make one another happy. In this belief he may in fact be mistaken, and their friends might convince him that he is mistaken. Bert might now no longer want to marry Angela. In each of these cases, the person has the want only because of false beliefs that he holds.

Obviously enough, the situation might not be quite so simple. Despite having been convinced that he cannot make Angela happy, Bert might still want to marry her anyway. In that case, his want to marry Angela is not based on the false belief that he held. Similarly,

John might say, 'Well, I'll try the penicillin then'. There may be some other false belief underlying *this* want (for example, that penicillin will cure his headache); but at any rate it will not be true that John wants the tablets on the table only because of his false belief that they are aspirin; or alternatively, it may be that that *was* why he wanted them, but is not why he wants them now. This latter is the more natural way to take the example; but we must not exclude the possibility that John felt so badly that he was willing to take any tablets that came to hand, whether or not they were aspirin as he believed.

It is to be noted that even when the want is based on a false belief, what was wanted might still have satisfied the desire in question. John's headache might have been caused by some infection which penicillin *would* have cured, and perhaps the tablets would therefore have got rid of his headache more effectively than aspirin would have done. But if John does not know this, or does not believe it, he may well no longer want the tablets once he has been told what they are. It is no part of my argument that wants based on false beliefs cannot lead to our desires being satisfied. The only criterion I wish to invoke is whether or not the person still wants the same thing once his false beliefs about it have been corrected.

It is quite often the case that we want things only because we hold false beliefs about them. In our past experience, we have ample evidence of this; and we must surely suppose that at least some of the things we at present want appeal to us because we hold false beliefs about them, although for the moment we have no means of discovering that our beliefs are false. So, we make many choices only on the basis of all kinds of false beliefs: about the education of our children, the choice of someone to marry, the treatment of disease, the management of the economy, the conduct of our personal relationships, and the way in which we try to help the Third World. Were all our beliefs about these topics correct, our conduct would in fact be, or have been, very different. As I have just indicated, it will not follow in every case that our desires were unsatisfied because of the false beliefs governing our wants; but it must be admitted that more of our desires would have been satisfied had all our wants been based on true beliefs.

We would not have had the tragedy of children crippled by thalido-mide administered to their mothers; we should have made a better job of the education of our children, a better choice of marriage partners, we should have avoided at least some of our economic crises, and so on. We are not yet in a position to give a complete account of the matter, but so far forth it seems undeniable that our knowledge of what our moral duty in fact was would have been much better had we held fewer false beliefs of a completely non-moral kind; and, to the extent that these beliefs determined our wants, our conduct would have been morally better as well, even though we might not be to blame for acting as we did.

Wants based on misinterpreted urges

The term 'urge' has been chosen because it is about as unspecific as it could be. I intend it to refer to the very basic drives possession of which is part of what we mean by being a human being. I take it to be a conceptual truth that all men have the same urges. Exactly which these are is a matter for psychological theory to determine. But I hope it is reasonably uncontroversial to point to the drives connected with food, sex, self-preservation, the giving and receiving of affection, aggression, the acquisition of knowledge, and, perhaps, the playing of a definite role in society. Urges are comparatively unspecific; wants, on the other hand, are much more specific ways in which we give expression to and interpret the urges we have. Whereas urges are innate, wants are learnt, and are learnt very differently according to the culture in which we grow up and live. We have learnt to want and find satisfying very different kinds of food, very different ways of defending our interests, or manifesting affection; we have learnt to look for support from very different groups of people, to be interested in very different areas of know-ledge, and so on. Even when two wants are related to the same urge they may not be readily interchangeable. Thus, I may be quite unable to eat and retain food which another person would regard as a great delicacy and which is in fact highly nutritious.

It is not always easy for us to interpret our urges in terms of wants, particularly highly specific wants. Misinterpretation is always possible. The test for misinterpretation which I propose is as follows: a want is a misinterpretation of the relevant urge when, once we have got what we wanted, we remain unsatisfied. Consider the following example. Tom is feeling out of sorts and miserable. He tells himself that what he wants is to get himself organized and do some serious work. But in the act of setting out his books and papers he comes to realize that that is not going to help. Perhaps a change of scene and some relaxation? But even as he makes his way towards the cinema, he becomes aware that he is going to feel just as out of sorts there as he did at home. A walk in the fresh air? But after an hour or so walking in the park, he feels no better. It is only when he has returned disconsolately home that he finds to his delight that an old friend has called unexpectedly. They spend an enjoyable evening together.

In this example, Tom was in some way dissatisfied, and endeavoured to interpret his dissatisfaction in terms of a series of wants. As it turned out, none of his efforts succeeded in identifying which urge was involved, or what was required to meet the desires connected with it. In the end, that he really needed company was a conclusion which he arrived at fortuitously. Of course, this is not always so, but it serves to make the point that correct identification is not always easy to achieve even when we want to; and there may well be unacknowledged psychological causes which inhibit clarity, and which represent yet further urges which ought to be taken into account. We are here dealing with an immensely complex set of interrelated urges and desires and the wants in which we give them expression; some of these are highly specific (I want a large steak), others more general (I want my family to be happy) and others extremely general, for which we may not even have words. In the case of some of the wants we have, we have a pretty clear idea of the relationship between our wants and the urges on which they are ultimately based; in other cases, if we can believe the psychologists, this relationship is not readily accessible to us – for instance, exactly why is it that someone wants a cigarette? The possibilities of misidentification are therefore very considerable, and it seems to me that a great deal of human unhappiness stems from the pursuit of wants which are based on misinterpretations of this kind. People change their jobs when it is really their marriages which need attention, or drink excessively when their real need is for affection, or less responsibility, or a challenge in their job. I need not multiply examples.

I have already noted that an urge which is common to all men can in different cultures be given a very wide range of satisfactory interpretations. People have learnt to want very different things, and there is no reason to suppose that different cultures, each based on a different set of learnt wants, cannot offer equally fulfilling ways of life. It is no part of the view I am advocating that there should be only one correct interpretation of a given urge. Nor do I see any need to assume that for a given individual in a given culture there is only one set of wants in the satisfaction of which his happiness must lie. On the contrary, I should imagine that all of us could achieve happiness in a number of ways, and that we might even learn to be happy in some very unfamiliar ways. I wish to argue only that this variety does not mean that all the things we say we want are capable of satisfying us, and that one of the reasons for this is that those wants on occasion misinterpret the urges which are at the core of our human nature.

Wants which are incompossible

Both at any particular moment, and over a period of time or even a lifetime, we want things which cannot be jointly obtained. One person may be unable both to spend the Easter vacation at a ski-resort and to pass his examinations in June; another may be unable both to reach the top of his profession and devote his time to his family; another may be unable to spend money now and provide for his old age. It may be impossible for us to have both a stable currency and full employment. Yet, taken singly, these wants might involve neither of the two kinds of mistake we have considered in the preceding sections.

I shall term wants which cannot both be met incompossible wants. We may, or may not, be aware of the incompossibility of the various wants which we entertain, but the incompossibility will remain whether we are aware of it or not. It may be that simply to become aware of the incompossibility of two wants will have the effect of altering one of them; if a man really becomes aware that his ambitions are threatening his marriage, he may find that his love for his wife is such that he simply loses interest in the promotion ladder. More commonly, I suspect, the mere recognition that two wants are incompossible will not of itself have the effect of making us less inclined to either of the things we want. Still, no rational justification can be given for an action in terms of an incompossible set of wants. If we take the wants as a set, there is, by definition, no action which can be justified as a means to the complex goal defined in terms of that set. If we take the wants individually, a particular action will turn out to be justified in terms of one want, and unjustified in terms of the other.

Obviously enough, some kind of choice is required in the case of incompossible wants. One has to be sacrificed to the other, or, possibly, modifications must be made in both in such a way that the new set of wants is now compossible. Is there anything which can be said about the constraints which should be placed on such choices?

Bentham suggests that, other things being equal, there is more to be gained by choosing that alternative to which one is more inclined, or for which one has the greater desire. Despite the difficulties involved in quantifying desires, it seems to me that this is a plausible suggestion. But there are (as Bentham himself would admit) many other qualifications which must be made. For instance, it may well be the case that the incompossibility arises between a present want and a future one, as when expenditure now excludes making provision for one's old age. In this kind of case, the person simply may not feel inclined at all to make provision for his old age, although he may know that he will at some future date feel inclined to benefit from the provision which has been made. So at any rate the strength of present inclinations is not a reasonable guide. It may also be that to speak of the 'strength' of inclinations, while a reasonable metaphor in some cases, is misleading in others, and it would be more natural simply to ask what alternative one prefers.

There is also a different kind of constraint which might be mentioned. Perhaps one should opt for that alternative which in turn will pose the fewest further problems of incompossibility with other wants which one has. Again, other things being equal, I believe that there is much to be said for this suggestion. More generally, I think it can be said that, other things being equal, it is preferable to learn to interpret one's urges in such a way that the learnt wants which one has pose the fewest problems of incompossibility one with another. To take the (probably unrealizable) limiting case: if all the wants which one had learnt were compossible, it would be possible (leaving other people out of account, for the moment) to satisfy all one's desires, and it would seem that this was preferable to a situation in which one was forced to choose between them.

On the other hand, I do not think it can be assumed that it is always preferable to opt for that one of a pair of incompossible wants which poses the fewest further problems of incompossibility. It may be that I much prefer the alternative, and would be prepared to sacrifice many other wants in order to achieve this one. I shall try to say something more on this when discussing pluralism and relativism in ethics in Chapter IV. For the moment, the only point on which I wish to insist is that no choice can be justified if the agent in fact is operating with an incompossible set of wants. Given the inadequacy of our knowledge of future events, and of our own future development, it is in practice inevitable that we will in fact have incompossible wants which we do not at the moment know to be incompossible. Moreover, I think it is not uncommon for us to have here and now wants which we suspect to be incompossible, or even know to be incompossible, and yet for us to try to conceal this incompossibility from ourselves. We obviously have motives for trying to persuade ourselves that it is possible for us to have our cake and eat it. The point of this filter is to exclude those wants which belong to an incompossible set. We will not be able to operate this filter with one hundred percent efficiency, it is true; but I suggest that, to the extent that we can operate it at all, it will make a big difference to the way in which we behave.

Rational needs

This section might equally have been entitled 'Needs': but for the sake of clarity, I have inserted the word 'rational' to underline that I take the needs in question to be true, genuine, and rationally defensible, and not merely apparent or alleged needs. I propose, then, to define as a rational need any want which satisfies all the following criteria:

(a) it is not based on a false belief;

(b) it is not based on a misinterpreted urge;

(c) it is not part of a set of wants which are jointly incompossible;

(d) the set of wants of which it is a member *either* is maximally compossible, *or* has been deliberately chosen in preference to such a set.

To some extent the ground has already been cleared for the fourth of these criteria, but it perhaps requires some additional justification. The problem, as I see it, is to exclude that class of wants which we might normally incline to describe as 'neurotic' or 'psychotic' in such a way that one neither simply begs the question in their regard, nor excludes them in such a way as also to exclude all other ways of life in which many inclinations are sacrificed for the sake of one or two dominating goals.

Let me take a reasonably uncontroversial example of a desire which would normally be described as neurotic. Jemima wants to wash her hands a large number of times each day — say, every hour at least, and sometimes more often than that. Let us now consider how this desire would fare when tested by the criteria I have proposed. There need not, so far as I can see, be any false belief involved in it. Nor can it be shown to be a misinterpretation of any urge, since the criterion for something being a misinterpretation is that obtaining what is wanted leaves the person dissatisfied. But in fact Jemima feels very much better as soon as she has washed her hands; indeed, I take it that a psychologist might say that she has developed this pattern of behaviour precisely because it *does* succeed in making her feel better. To be sure, the malaise returns quickly enough, and the pattern of hand-washing has to be repeated. But that is not of itself evidence of misinterpretation as I have defined it, any more than the fact that I will still be hungry for lunch a few hours after eating breakfast is evidence that my wanting to have breakfast is a misinterpretation of my urge for food. It is tempting to argue that what Jemima *really* wants is, let us say, affection and security, or freedom from guilt, and to try to show in this way that her wanting to wash her hands is a misinterpretation of the urge in question. But my account of misinterpretation is not strong enough to support this argument, for the reason I have just given; moreover, it would be very difficult to strengthen it to meet this point without producing even more serious difficulties elsewhere. We do not want so to define misinterpretation as to predetermine which set of learnt wants are admissible just because we disapprove of some learnt wants and not others. We do not wish, for example, to have to allow the argument that someone who devotes all his time and resources to sailing round the world single-handed really should have learnt a more balanced set of wants.

To return to Jemima. It certainly is the case that she has had many problems of incompossibility to overcome: she has to spend large sums on handcream which she would have liked to spend on other things; she is embarrassed by her frequent exits from social gatherings, and in the end has decided to refuse many invitations she would otherwise have wished to accept. Certain types of job are just not realistic possibilities for her. Still, she has now so arranged things that her wants, now, are so far as she can see a compossible set. In short, Jemima's desire to wash her hands passes the first three criteria quite successfully.

We may assume for the purposes of this discussion that Jemima's desire for hand-washing is connected with much more basic desires for affection and security. We may also assume that it either is, or at some time in her childhood was, possible for her to have learnt other ways of satisfying her desire for security which would not have posed such severe problems of incompossibility with respect to the other wants which she has. Her present set of wants is not, or at least was not, maximally compossible, and therefore fails the first part of the fourth criterion. However, I think it quite arguable that the desire to spend one's life sailing round the world single-handed would also fail this test. What is wanted is some further test which Jemima will still fail, but which the single-handed yachtsman will pass. In this spirit, I propose the second part of the fourth criterion. Jemima fails, since I take it that she was unable to resolve the incompossibilities in any other way; whereas the yachtsman deliberately decided to subordinate other desires to his desire to sail round the world, and so his desire to do so will pass the test I proposed. I would hope to deal with all 'neurotic' or 'psychotic' wants in a similar way.

I now wish to maintain that none of these tests by which certain wants are filtered out begs any morally important question. At least there are some well-known pitfalls into which the tests do not fall. No want has been excluded on the grounds that it is a lower rather than a higher want; nor on the grounds that morally respectable people do not have wants like that; nor that some wants are known in advance to be morally disreputable, or in some other way morally undesirable. The guiding principle behind the tests I propose could be expressed as follows. If it is true that human welfare has something to do with the satisfaction of wants, then it will take no account of wants which are in some sense or other self-defeating. I have therefore tried to spell out various ways in which getting what one wants is still in some way unsatisfying. The criteria are based on the nature of wanting itself, rather than on any moral judgment about the content of what is wanted. I think similar criteria could be defended in the context of playing chess.

It is only the fourth criterion whose moral neutrality could, I think, be seriously questioned. It might well be alleged that the second leg of this criterion displays an unargued moral preference for deliberate choices. While I think this is true, I do not think that it totally destroys the argument I have presented. In the first place, the proposed criterion is still neutral in that it does not determine *which* deliberate choice ought to be made. Suppose Jemima *deliberately* chose frequent hand-washing as a way of life instead of other ways of living open to her. On my criterion, there would be nothing to criticize in this choice, any more than in the choice of the yachtsman, and I think this is as it should be. Secondly, I think that my admitted preference for deliberate policies in life at the expense of ones which are entered upon because of some compulsion is at least sufficiently uncontroversial that, if it is not conceded as morally neutral, I can still afford to make it simply an unargued assumption, adopted for the sake of its explanatory power.

I wish further to claim that it is plausible to say that those wants which survive all four tests are genuine needs, and that other wants are not. I hope that the criteria I propose provide a clear decision-procedure for discriminating between the various wants that we have. Of course, it will not always be possible for us to have all the knowledge which is required in order to sort out our wants with certainty. Our knowledge of the world, and our knowledge of ourselves is to a greater or lesser extent incomplete, and without this knowledge the four tests I propose cannot be completely carried out. Nevertheless, these tests show clearly the direction in which progress can be made, and this is all that can be expected of a moral theory.

Morally Relevant Values

If this much is granted, I now propose to offer a definition of a morally relevant value, or something which is good from the moral point of view, in terms of the preceding account of rational needs. I shall use 'good' as a convenient abbreviation for 'morally relevant value'.

> *'Something is good' = df 'It is capable of satisfying a rational need'*

I shall argue later that this definition will enable us to give an account of the emotive or commendary force of 'good' which has, I think rightly, been stressed by Stevenson and Hare in their different ways. But in what sense, if any, is the proposed definition naturalist? It is certainly not the case that an evaluative term is being defined in non-evaluative terms, for 'rational need' is, I think, doubly evaluative. Plainly, 'rational' as I am using it refers to an evaluation of the various wants we have. It also seems to me that the term 'need', like 'want' is both factual and evaluative; factual, since it is a matter of empirical inquiry whether or not someone has a particular want; and evaluative in that to want something is not an evaluatively-neutral attitude to have towards that thing. If naturalism consists in defining values in terms of facts, then my proposed definition is not naturalist. On the other hand, it is sometimes held that naturalism consists in defining moral words in terms of non-moral words. In this sense, my definition is intended to be naturalist, for it is my contention that no moral considerations are involved in determining what a rational need is, whereas 'good' is, at least in a wider sense, plainly a moral term.

I have already argued that no logical fallacy is involved in a naturalist definition of this kind. And if, as I have argued above, it is true that morality is essentially connected with human welfare, and human welfare in turn is connected with the satisfaction of human desires, there can surely be no general objection to defining a moral term like 'good' in such a way as to relate it to a particular sub-set of human desires. Nor can it be urged against this definition that it begs all the important moral questions at the outset, for the term 'rational' has been elaborated without any moral assumptions (or, at least, without any *controversial* moral assumptions) being made. It also seems to me that this definition does explain in simple, coherent, and clear terms, the beliefs that we have about which things are good, and in so doing represents a first step in explaining our moral notions more generally. I therefore offer it as the basic element in a moral theory, and as one which has the advantage of integrating morality with our knowledge of ourselves and our environment.

Some further advantages of this definition are immediately evident. On this view, morally relevant goods will involve a very wide range of human needs. It will not be the case that there is a stress on biological as distinct from, say, interpersonal needs, nor will there be any room for the kind of cultural imperialism which suggests that there is only one way in which human beings may legitimately find a satisfying way of life. Implicit in this definition is the view that human nature, and in particular human psychology, is extremely complex, and the variety of ways in which human beings can find fulfilment is correspondingly large. It also follows from this definition that moral knowledge presupposes knowledge of the world in which we live. We need to know which beliefs of a quite non-moral kind are true and which are false before we can know which things are good and can rationally be wanted. Claims to moral knowledge will be unwarranted to the extent that they go beyond the best factual knowledge available in, say, economics, or psychology, and the informal knowledge available to us outside the scientific field. Again, progress in moral knowledge will presuppose a willingness to step back from the desires of the moment, and to examine the structure of our pattern of wants as a whole.

I shall conclude this chapter with some disclaimers. It would be most unfortunate if the fact that I have based an account of good-ness on a theory of desires were to give the impression that I thought that a moral theory were egoistic in character, and still less that it would lead to selfishness. I would wish to insist that the moral duties which we have should take the needs of others into account just as much as our own. Selfishness, I take it, consists precisely in pursuing one's own interests at the expense of others in an illegitimate way. There is nothing in what I have said so far which leads to any such conclusion. Indeed, there is nothing which leads even to the conclusion that a person's wants are all directed towards himself. The issues here are more complex than they appear at first sight; but at any rate on an ordinary common sense level, I take it as obvious that people frequently want the welfare of others: a mother wants her children to be happy, a friend wants his friend to succeed, a man can be passionately involved in the betterment of the underprivileged; perhaps all of us need to be able to love others for their own sake in order to be fulfilled ourselves as human beings. It is not my purpose here to argue whether it is true, and in what sense, that all men have desires such as those I have just mentioned. But certainly there is nothing in what I have said which would suggest that they have not; and if they have, then I do not see why some of the objects of those desires should not be good.[11]

I have so far outlined only the first step in what I take to be a moral theory, in outlining a theory of morally relevant values. So far, nothing has been said about our moral obligations. I have not so far argued about which *actions* are right and which actions are wrong. I shall argue in the next chapter that 'right' and 'wrong' have in turn to be defined in terms of the relationship between actions and the values which I have argued for above. Roughly, we will be obliged to act in such a way as to satisfy the rational needs of as many people as possible. But such an account, even if it is true so far as it goes, is seriously incomplete. All would be well, provided that people's rational needs were never incompossible with those of other people, and provided also that we were never

---

[11] See further Kenny (1), and Gosling.

faced with a choice about whose needs to satisfy, given that we were not able to satisfy everyone's. Now, it is my view that very many of our everyday moral problems involve situations where the interests of the various people concerned in fact coincide. Thus it is often the case that any given member of a family will be fulfilled only to the extent that the other members of the family are too. The idea that I can be happy and that my true needs can be satisfied without those with whom I am most closely involved being equally happy and satisfied may, on occasions, be seductive; but I think it is usually false. Nonetheless, we are on occasions forced to choose between people who cannot all have their true needs met, just as we are forced to choose between incompossible wants of our own. It is the function of a theory of justice to guide such choices. Notoriously, the theory of justice is extremely controversial, and I do not know of any wholly satisfactory way of constructing one. I do not offer one here. I would, however, insist that any viable theory of justice can be built only on a knowledge of the true needs that people have.

The aim of this chapter has been to lay the groundwork of the moral theory to which appeal must ultimately be made in the attempt to justify any of our moral judgments. One result of the argument has been to show that such a theory must, in the end, rest on a vast body of purely factual knowledge about our own human nature, and the world in which we have to live. Without such knowledge, the theory itself will have no substantive content. In this sense, the ultimate court of appeal in ethics is to the facts — the ordinary non-moral facts learnt through our scientific and informal reflection on our non-moral experience. It is in this body of knowledge, so far as I can see, that the ultimate authority in ethics must lie. Because they insist on this, natural law theories of ethics, however mistaken they may be or have been in other respects, are decisively better than their theological competitors.

III

The Authority of Moral Principles

The conclusions so far reached have an important bearing on the way in which moral principles might be said to have authority. Consequently, what I have said so far has implications for the way in which moral principles should be appealed to in the process of ethical argument. In particular, it might be held that moral principles, or at least some moral principles, have enormous authority, because they state moral truths which are in some sense absolute; and from this it might be argued that the correct method to follow in a moral discussion consists in identifying the relevant moral principle, and acting upon it. Partly as a reaction to this way of looking at the matter, some moralists have regarded moral principles as constituting a kind of threat to the autonomy of the individual, and a willingness to appeal to such principles as a kind of moral infantilism. These are the issues which will principally concern us in this chapter. But there are several prior questions which must be discussed before the more central issues can be approached. The notions of intrinsic value and absolute value need to be examined, as does the relationship between these notions and the corresponding ideas of obligation.

Intrinsic Value and Intrinsic Obligation

I propose to use the term 'intrinsic value' to refer to the value which something has just because of what it is, without regard to what else might follow from it or be produced by it. This will serve to contrast intrinsic value with instrumental value, while leaving it for the moment an open question whether or not things which are intrinsically valuable are also absolutely valuable. Now, it has already been argued that value (at least those values which are morally relevant) is connected with the satisfaction of a rational human need. Those things, events, states of affairs, actions and activities are valuable which are related to the satisfaction of rational needs. It will be recalled that it makes no difference, for the moment, *whose* needs are in question; nor is it presupposed that all a person's needs are for his own well-being, or his own gratification.

There are very many kinds of objects which can be the object of a rational need. We can need things like books and food, institutions like universities or the legal system, events such as passing examinations, or a period of fine weather, and so on. It is surely too all-embracing to suggest that all these are intrinsically valuable. A first step in narrowing down the list might be to suggest that only those objects of rational needs are intrinsically valuable which are also states or activities of persons. In making this suggestion, we might have in mind states like being healthy, or well-educated, and activities such as learning, praying, playing football, or just simply relaxing, as well as more complex activities like loving or experiencing sympathy for someone. The suggestion is helpful so far as it goes, I think, but it certainly does not take us all the way. There are many states and activities of persons which we would not want to say were valuable in themselves but which still might be the object of a rational need. Taking exercise, for example, need not be intrinsically valuable, and it might even be argued that not all instances of learning are intrinsically valuable either. We can, of course, suggest that only those states or activities of persons are intrinsically valuable which are wanted for their own sake. The trouble with this suggestion is that it does not enable us to identify in advance which things are intrinsically valuable. It has been shown, for instance, that even such candidates as 'pleasure' or 'enjoyment' cannot in any simple or unified sense be said to be the only things which we want for their own sakes. Nevertheless, I can see no other way of delimiting in a concrete way the list of things which are intrinsically valuable, and I think we must be content with saying that any state or activity of a person is intrinsically valuable if it is the object of a rational need, and if the person is willing to say that he wants it for its own sake.

Suppose we now ask whether *actions* can be intrinsically valuable? If we extend the term 'action' to include activities, such as praying, or showing affection, or playing a game, then it seems to me that actions can be intrinsically valuable. In other words, engaging in these activities just for their own sake is something which is a good thing in a sense of 'good' which is a properly moral sense.

For the most part, actions are not like this. Most of the things we do are done not for their own sake, but for the sake of some result which can be brought about by acting in these ways. Thus, we get dressed, add up accounts, get on trains, write books, buy groceries, work at our jobs. We can hope that these actions have instrumental value, without committing ourselves to the view that they necessarily, or usually, have any intrinsic value.

Terminology is important here. It is possible to speak of what we do as an action, and to contrast this action with the various descriptions we might give of it. Alternatively, (and I shall adopt this convention, without here discussing the merits of two different approaches to action-theory) we might say that actions are both identified and individuated by their descriptions, and adopt some more neutral term for what these descriptions are descriptions of. I shall speak of pieces of behaviour (without giving any technical sense to 'behaviour' other than to assume that the behaviour in question will be voluntary), and I shall refer to that behaviour under a particular description as an 'action'. On this view, then, I shall speak of 'causing pain', 'pulling a tooth' and 'curing a toothache' as three different actions, even though, evidently, these could each be true descriptions of the one piece of behaviour.

Quite in general, there is therefore a need for us to be able to identify which action(s) a person is performing when he is behaving in a particular way. In part, we learn to do this just by learning to use the action-words in our language. We learn to use expressions such as 'walking' or 'writing' or 'drawing' or 'playing a game', although I do not believe that learning to use these expressions necessarily, or indeed usually, involves being able to give precise definitions of them. In addition, we learn which of several possible correct action-descriptions of a piece of behaviour is the appropriate one to use in different circumstances; the opera singer is singing a Mozart aria, and is not normally said to be making noises with her voice, nor trying to sing a Mozart aria as best she can, even though it may be that, from one point of view or another, each of these descriptions of what she is doing would be a correct one. Once again, I do not think that it is in general possible to give a neutral and complete account of 'appropriate' in connection with appropriate descriptions of behaviour.[1]

What is true of actions in general is also, I think, true of those actions considered from the point of view of ethical theory. We need to be able to know how to characterize people's behaviour from the moral point of view. Thus we need to know when it is proper to say that someone killed someone, or stole something, or behaved unprofessionally or told a lie. But I think it impossible to give an account of our ability to use these terms as though this ability depended on the use of precise and morally neutral definitions of them. The most that an ethical theory can be expected to do, I think, is to give some account of the framework of discourse within which such terms are applied to behaviour, and I shall outline the first steps in so doing later in this essay. It must be stressed, however, that no such outline of the framework will ever provide a set of necessary and sufficient conditions for the use of our moral words. This is a feature of our use of language quite generally, and not a peculiarity of moral language as such.

Although the action-terms which we use to characterize behaviour are in this way open-textured, it seems to me that once we have identified a piece of behaviour as an action of a particular type, we are then in a position to say something about the value of an action. We evaluate behaviour, I suggest, first of all by seeing that behaviour as an instance of a type of action. Although it is no doubt true that a piece of behaviour has the value it has independently of the way we describe it, we cannot specify even which piece of behaviour is being evaluated except by identifying it as an

[1]   See further D'Arcy, Goldman, and Anscombe (2).

action. In this sense, it seems to me that value belongs primarily to actions as such, and to behaviour only in an extrapolated and theoretical sense. Thus, if what that man is doing is causing someone pain, it seems to me that his action is bad; if, on the other hand, he is pulling a tooth, it might be argued that that action as such is neither good nor bad: or perhaps more plausibly, that that action, too, is bad; but if he is curing a toothache, then that action is good. To ask whether what he is doing is good or bad is to ask a question to which no answer can be given independently of an answer to the question about how his behaviour is to be classified.

I propose, then, to say that actions are intrinsically valuable when their descriptions either are descriptions of intrinsically valuable activities, or else involve descriptions of intrinsically valuable states of persons. This will have to be modified presently, but we may consider some simpler cases first. For some agents, then, though not necessarily for all, such actions as sailing a dinghy on holiday, praying and learning about philosophy will be intrinsically valuable. So will the actions of giving pleasure to one's friends, curing someone's illness, teaching, and showing sympathy. Similarly, causing someone pain, hurting someone's feelings, making someone ill, and refusing to satisfy a genuine need will be intrinsically disvaluable.

Two modifications must be made in this account. It may well be that the description of an action contains reference both to intrinsically valuable and to intrinsically disvaluable states of the persons involved. A simple example might be the action 'smacking the child to teach it not to play with the electric fire', where there is a reference both to the child's pain and to the growth in the child's knowledge. A more complex example might be 'sacrificing one's own life and thereby enabling others to escape', where there is reference both to the expression of love, the death of the agent, and the safety of others. Where the action performed is complex, the process of evaluating that action will be similarly complex. Once again we are faced with the same kind of problem we encountered earlier when we considered the necessity of choosing between incompossible desires. Some preference must come into play, but it is not immediately clear *which* preference. So too here, in order to evaluate such actions we will have to decide whether it is preferable for a child to learn not to play with the fire, or preferable that it should not have the pain of being smacked. So far, I have said no more than that I see no general way of establishing that there is only one defensible order of preferences in terms of which such actions can be evaluated, although there are some general considerations which might place some constraints on our preferences in certain types of case.

The second modification concerns such actions as 'breaking a promise'. I would like to tackle this by considering an action like 'being unfair'. I have already expressed the view that a fully developed theory of obligation will have to include some theory of justice which tells us how to act in cases where different people have incompossible desires and we have to choose which person to satisfy. Implicit in this view is the view that justice or fairness is not itself a moral *value*, as I have defined that term, although it is plainly connected with moral values, and is itself a moral obligation. In the same way, I would not wish to say that 'breaking a promise' was in itself an intrinsically disvaluable action, although it seems to me arguable that it might violate an obligation.

It will be convenient to continue the discussion of the terms 'intrinsic' and 'absolute' in terms of obligations rather than in terms of values, although most of what I have to say could apply equally well to both. Accordingly, I must say something about the relationship which I take to hold between values and obligations generally.

Theories of obligation frequently operate with three categories of action: obligatory, wrong, and permissible. On this view, it will be possible to perform an action which is permissible and not obligatory. Thus, in the Christian moral tradition, it has commonly been held that the practice of the evangelical counsels of perfection is permissible, but not obligatory; it would be equally permissible for someone to choose to live a good Christian life without practising them. And in general, one could not be blamed for doing a good action, even if it was not the best possible action that one could have performed at the time. The alternative to this view is the view taken by the classical utilitarians (although one does not have to be a utilitarian to hold it), that one's obligation is to perform the best action available. To perform an action which, albeit good, is not the best that one could have done is, on this view, wrong. In my opinion, there is much to be said for this second way of looking at obligations. It is difficult to find any justification for doing what is second-best; and there is a strong Christian tradition according to which one has a duty to strive for perfection in one's actions. To be sure, naïve and incautious attempts to apply this principle have often led to a rigorism which has had very damaging effects. Someone working with rigid and unexamined ideas of what the most perfect action available to him actually is can commit himself to behaviour which leads to stress, insensitivity, and even to the neglect of the most obvious duties. Cases of this kind do not invalidate the general view that one's duty is to do the best available action. They simply serve to point the moral that one ought to be extremely careful in making the assessment of what the best action actually is, in the light of its actual effects and of one's own capabilities. On balance, then, I think it is preferable to work with a two-valued theory of obligation, in which an action is either obligatory or wrong in the individual case, and to use 'right' as a synonym for 'obligatory'. I shall conduct the remainder of this discussion on that assumption; but I think that what I have to say could be adapted reasonably easily to accommodate a three-valued theory of obligation should this be thought preferable.

Although actions will be right or wrong according to the relationship they have to intrinsically valuable or disvaluable states, it will therefore not be sufficient to show that an action is instrumentally or intrinsically good in order to establish that it is right. Nor, to establish that it is wrong, will it be sufficient to establish that it is instrumentally or intrinsically bad. There are two reasons for this. Firstly, for an action to be right, it will have to be the best of the good actions one could have performed; and if none of the actions open to one was good, then it will suffice that it is the least bad. Secondly, one must take into account the claims of justice. In short, we have a moral duty to act in such a way that as many human beings as possible reach their fulfilment conformably to the demands of justice, and to avoid actions which achieve less than this.

It is a corollary of this view of obligation that it will frequently be unclear to us what we ought to do, in the fullest sense of 'ought'. In order to be clear about our obligations, we should have to be clear about just what the effects will be if we behave in a particular way. For example, it may well be impossible for us to determine in advance the effects of sending a child to this school rather than to that, or of embarking on a particular career rather than some other which was open to us, or of taking immediate measures to reflate the economy. The effects of these actions on the welfare of the persons they affect may well be to a greater or lesser extent hidden from us. Even with hindsight we may not always be in a position to know what we ought to have done; for although it may be clear enough that what we did worked out badly (or well enough), it may still be difficult to say whether some alternative might not have worked out worse (or much better still).

For the most part we have to be content with a less demanding notion of obligation, where 'ought' is defined not in terms of what is actually achieved by an action, but in terms of the best available evidence concerning our actions. This need not paralyse us into inactivity; it is simply part of our human condition that we must frequently act in ignorance, and we must just make the best of it. On the other hand, sketching out a theory of what we ideally 'ought' to do is not an otiose activity. It has the important function of indicating the direction in which greater moral knowledge lies.

The theory of obligation which I propose, then, states that in order to assess whether an action is right or wrong, we must look at what is achieved by that action, both in itself and in its results. The theory of morally relevant values already given enables us to assess the value of the various activities and states of affairs involved in our actions in terms of the satisfaction of rational needs. The advantage of this view is that it tells us just what to look for when we try to assess our actions morally, even if it holds out no guarantee that ideally correct answers will always be available. I submit that only this way of considering questions of rightness and wrongness accounts for what we experience as the complexity of many of our moral decisions, while still giving us the key with which we can begin to make progress in dealing with that complexity. Other types of moral theory seem to me to fall into one of two opposing errors: either they ignore the complexity altogether, by suggesting that ideally correct answers are available without the need for the complex empirical inquiry into the effects of our actions on the welfare of human beings; or else, bewildered by the difficulties, they abandon rational inquiry altogether by suggesting that we simply have to decide what to do in each situation, and that that decision is beyond any rational criticism. The first view seems to me to be *a priori* nonsense; and the second some kind of situationalist anarchy.

Against this background we may now ask whether actions can be intrinsically right or wrong. If we ask this question of a particular piece of behaviour, we can see quite easily that a piece of behaviour will be intrinsically right or wrong just because it is the behaviour it is, with the effects that it has. There is much to be said for the medieval view held by Aquinas[2] that *all* individual pieces of behaviour will be intrinsically right or wrong, since no matter what piece of behaviour will have some effect on someone's welfare. Be that as it may, the conclusion that pieces of behaviour can be intrinsically right or wrong is quite unilluminating. What we really wish to know is whether *types* of behaviour, actions, can be intrinsically right or wrong; for once we know this, we can say something systematic about them. Once again we are confronted with the fact that actions are identified by the way in which they are described, and their rightness and wrongness will depend on this fact.

I think three categories of actions must be considered. With an eye to the conclusions I hope to establish, I shall classify them as A-type, P-type, and F-type actions respectively; 'A' will stand for 'absolute', 'P' for *'prima facie'*, and 'F' for 'factual'. It may be helpful to keep these labels in mind throughout the discussion, although their justification will be clear only as the argument proceeds. Consider, then, three types of action, identified by the following descriptions of a person's behaviour:

> A. To commit murder
> To apportion benefits justly
> To be loving

[2]   S.T. I–II, 18, 8 and 9.

P. To cause someone pain
    To kill someone
    To feed the hungry
    To keep a promise
    To get an education

F. To catch a train
    To build a house
    To pay someone £100 per week

Obviously enough, any piece of behaviour which is described in terms of an A-type action will also be describable in terms of some F-type action and in terms of some P-type actions as well. Thus, if Bert has murdered Bill, it will also be true that he has killed him, and also that he (for instance) fired a bullet in Bill's direction, fired a gun, pulled a trigger, and so on. Further, a piece of behaviour described in terms of an F-type action may also be describable in terms of some P-type action, and perhaps also in terms of an A-type action; if we ask what Andrew is doing, it may be true that he is paying Albert £100 per week, that he is keeping a promise to Albert, and that he is behaving justly towards Albert. If we ask whether an action is intrinsically right, we are already talking about a type of behaviour, and the answer will depend to some extent on whether the behaviour is an instance of A-type, P-type, or F-type behaviour. On the other hand, if one asks whether what someone is doing is intrinsically right, one will first have to establish which description of what he is doing is the proper one to use in describing it. I shall elaborate each of these two points in turn.

Suppose, for the moment, that a piece of behaviour is legitimately described as an A-type action. Two conclusions can be drawn: firstly, the action is right or wrong just because it is the kind of action that it is; and, secondly, that there is nothing more from the moral point of view which needs to be said about the behaviour in question. That these actions are intrinsically right or wrong is clear enough; in the case of murder, there is an immediate connection with an intrinsically disvaluable state of affairs, and in the case of being loving there is an activity which is in itself an intrinsically good activity; and in the case of behaving justly, although the connection between justice and *value* is not a simple one, justice is itself a basic type of obligation. The second conclusion is more open to dispute, however, at least in the cases of justice and being loving, if not in the case of murder. Once it is agreed that the proper description of someone's behaviour is that he murdered someone else, there is by definition no further moral qualification which can be added which could affect the wrongness of what he did. Considerations tending to show that an act of killing was not wrong would automatically tend to show that it was not murder either. The case of behaving justly is ambiguous. In Aristotle's general sense of 'justice' (which is also one of the main biblical senses) the word refers not to the exercise of one particular virtue, or the fulfilment of one particular type of obligation (which might then be contrasted with clemency, for example), but to right action in general. To behave justly in this sense simply is to behave rightly, and any consideration tending to show that the action was not right would tend also to show that it was not just. Similar considerations apply to some more recent Christian uses of 'to be loving', reflecting the great commandment of the Gospel in which is summed up all the law and the prophets. In the case of A-descriptions, then, we can say that the actions identified by them are intrinsically right or wrong, as the case may be, and that nothing more needs to be said. On the other hand, this latter assertion masks the fact that the really controversial issue is already assumed to have been settled. The real difficulty lies not in saying that murder is intrinsically wrong and that there is no more to be said; it lies in determining whether it is proper to describe a particular piece of behaviour as murder.

P-type actions are different from A-type actions in one respect, and not in the other. Like A-type actions, P-type actions are intrinsically right or wrong just because of the kind of actions they are; either they are immediately connected with valuable or disvaluable states of persons, or (as in the case of promising) they are instances of obligations in justice. On the other hand, P-type actions differ from A-type actions in that more than one P-type description may be applicable to what someone did, and these descriptions may be of opposite quality from the point of view of one's moral obligations. Suppose that Bert killed Bill; it may also be true that Bert was doing his duty as a soldier, or that he was defending his wife and children against Bill's threatening assaults. Again, Joan may have kept her promise to meet Peter at the cinema; but it may also be true that she left her critically ill mother unattended for three hours. Unlike the case of A-type actions, one and the same piece of behaviour may be an instance of several different P-type actions of opposite moral quality, each of which is nevertheless intrinsically right or wrong. In such cases, merely to identify someone's behaviour as an instance of a P-type action will not suffice to enable us to say whether what that person did was intrinsically right or wrong. Killing someone is intrinsically wrong, just because it is the kind of action that it is; but what Bert did may not have been wrong, even though it was an instance of killing. Promise-keeping is intrinsically right, but that is not sufficient to show that Joan acted rightly just because her behaviour was an instance of promise-keeping. Of course, it need not be the case that several opposing P-descriptions can properly be given of a particular piece of behaviour. It may be true that Bert killed Bill, and that, from the moral point of view, there is no further description of his behaviour to be given. In that case (assuming, of course, that Bert's behaviour was intentional) we could also say that Bert murdered Bill. Similarly, if all that can be said morally about a piece of behaviour is that Joan kept her promise, then what she did was intrinsically right just because that type of action is intrinsically right, and there is no other P-type action which Joan also performed.

F-type actions are different again. Identifying a piece of behaviour in terms of an F-type action of itself does nothing to enable us to judge what effect that behaviour had on human welfare. Building a house may have the effect of giving shelter to the homeless, but it may also deprive people of the only recreational space available to them. Paying someone £100 per week may be paying a just wage; but (in these inflationary times) it may simply have the effect of forcing several people to live below the poverty line. F-type actions, because their descriptions contain no reference either to basic obligations in justice or to intrinsically valuable states or activities, are of themselves neither intrinsically right nor intrinsically wrong. To identify behaviour as an instance of an F-type action does not enable us to make any moral assessment of the rightness or wrongness of that behaviour.

There are indefinitely many F-type descriptions which can be given of what someone is doing. Thus, someone might be sitting down; but equally, it might be true that he is sitting down in an armchair on a Tuesday; that he is sitting at home; that he is talking to somebody else; that he is telling a joke about Irishmen; and so on. No list of such features, however long, will of itself enable us to make any moral assessment of what he is doing. To this extent the critics of naturalism are right, that no moral term can be defined simply as a conjunction of such factual terms. On the other hand, it is also true that all, or any, of these factual descriptions of his behaviour might well be relevant evidence on the basis of which we could justify other P-type or even A-type descriptions of what he was doing. What is required here is further knowledge about the connections between the F-type actions and human needs; for example, was he just relaxing? Did the Irish joke hurt the other person's feelings; if it was a Tuesday, was there in existence an agreement whereby he had contracted to be at work at that time? Was he ill? If we ask how ought behaviour to be described in order to be assessed morally, the only answer is that all those features and only those features are relevant which are connected with the satisfaction or frustration of people's needs.

To say this is not to prejudge in any way what the overall effect on our assessment will be, once all these features have been included. Thus, it may be that Bert killed Bill; but until we know whether any other P-type description is applicable to Bert's action, we cannot make any final moral assessment of what he did. Perhaps, for example in so doing he saved his own wife and children? Perhaps, to alter the case, he thereby obtained a great deal of money on which he lived happily ever after? Perhaps the doctor who performed an abortion thereby saved a marriage? Clearly enough, the additional information about the relationship between the behaviour and human needs will not in every case lead us to change our moral judgement about whether the behaviour was right or wrong. What cannot be said in advance, however, is that these features need not even be considered before we make a moral judgement on what was done.

So far, then, I have argued for the following conclusions:

(1) Actions which are identified by A-type or P-type descriptions are intrinsically right or wrong, as the case may be, because in these descriptions there is already contained a reference to human welfare or damage.

(2) These descriptions refer to types of action; it is a further and much more difficult question to determine whether a particular piece of behaviour is to count as an instance of a certain P-type or A-type action, and hence whether that piece of behaviour is to be described as right or wrong.

(3) F-type actions are neither intrinsically right nor intrinsically wrong. On the other hand, establishing that someone performed an F-type action will frequently be the first step in setting up the chain of evidence on which we will judge whether that person also performed a P-type or A-type action.

(4) In assessing a person's behaviour, we must at least consider all the P-type actions which truly describe that behaviour; or, in other words, we must consider all those features of what was done which refer to human needs, on the basis of which these actions are to be evaluated; we must also consider any P-type description which refers to an obligation in justice.

Absolute Rightness and Wrongness

A clear distinction must be drawn between the assertion that something is absolutely right or wrong, and the assertion that it is intrinsically right or wrong. I take the assertion that something is absolutely right or wrong to mean that it is right or wrong in all possible circumstances, and independently of any further consequences. Obviously, this will be true only of actions (*types* of behaviour), and not of individual pieces of behaviour as such. In this respect, 'absolute' and 'intrinsic' are clearly different. Moreover, it will be evident that an action can be intrinsically wrong (or right) without necessarily being absolutely wrong (or right); to break a promise, or to cause pain, are wrong just because they are the actions they are; but it is not the case that there are no circumstances in which a promise should be broken, or pain caused. It is to be noted, too, that in my definition I have spoken of *further* consequences; I intend this to be a convenient way of signalling that I am not making any particular assumptions about where the line between an action and its consequences ought to be drawn. So far as questions of morality are concerned, it is clear to me that decisions about where to draw the line are made on the basis of moral assumptions about the significance of certain types of behaviour (e.g. adultery, or stealing, or murder, or lying), and the permissibility of engaging in such behaviour for the sake of the consequences which might thereby be brought about. Thus, to take a fairly clear case, those cases of telling untruths which are deemed permissible because of their consequences are also cases in which many would hesitate to describe the action as lying at all. The point I wish to make is that, in describing an action as absolutely right or wrong, we must have *already* identified that action, and in so doing we will have already decided upon a certain way of discriminating between action and consequences in the behaviour in question. To ascribe absolute moral quality to that action is to say that it has that quality irrespective of any other consequences, or, more accurately, independently of any other features of the behaviour (whether consequential or circumstantial) apart from those already included in the description of the action in question.

We can say at once that those actions which are identified by A-descriptions are absolutely right/wrong, since *ex hypothesi,* there are no further features which will make any difference. To establish that a particular piece of behaviour is murder is precisely to have taken into account all the relevant features. Murder, then, is both intrinsically and absolutely wrong. On the other hand, this assertion is of comparatively little practical value, since the real moral problem consists in establishing that it is proper to consider a particular piece of behaviour as an instance of murder.

We can also say at once that no action identified by an F-description can be absolutely right/wrong, any more than it can be intrinsically right or wrong.

The interesting cases concern actions identified by P-descriptions. We have already seen that particular pieces of behaviour can be truly described on at least some occasions in terms of different P-descriptions. Thus, someone can simultaneously be killing someone else and defending his wife and family. Moreover, as in this example, the two actions are of opposite moral quality, one intrinsically right and the other intrinsically wrong. Remembering that we are working within a two-valued logic of obligation whereby in any given situation an action will be either obligatory or wrong, we can now formulate conditions for absolute rightness and wrongness in the following way. Suppose that A and B are two P-type actions:

Absolute Rightness

An action A will be absolutely right (absolutely obligatory) if, but only if,

Either (1) No other action B is morally more important than A,

Or (2) If some action B is morally more important than A, A and B are never incompossible in any given situation.

Absolute Wrongness

An action A will be absolutely wrong if, but only if,

Either (1) A is worse than any other action B,

Or (2) If some action B is worse than A, avoiding B is always compossible with avoiding A in any given situation.

Absolute rightness and absolute wrongness are quite parallel to one another; but the two conditions, (1) and (2), are of very different kinds in each case.

As an illustration of (1), we might suppose that someone holds that fidelity to their marriage is an absolute duty. If he believes that on the basis of (1), then he must believe that no other duty could ever be more important; consideration for his parents, prospects in his career, his love for someone other than his wife, all must be less important. Less important, too, must be such negative duties as avoiding killing someone, avoiding emotional damage to his children, and so on. Similarly, if someone believes that, for example, killing an innocent man is absolutely wrong, he must believe that this action is worse than any other, including such actions as failing to defend his wife and children, or ridding his country of a bloody dictatorship.

On the other hand, as an illustration of (2), it might be argued that in actual practice nobody could ever be in the situation of having to choose between fidelity to his wife and the emotional welfare of his children, or between defending his country and the killing of innocent people. It is, in theory, quite possible to hold that several types of action are absolutely right or wrong, and to hold furthermore that some of these are morally more important than others, provided one also holds that one will never be in a situation where one is forced to choose between such absolutes.

We may now ask whether there is any reason to believe that either (1) or (2) is actually satisfied. With a qualification to be mentioned presently, I think it is true that no logically consistent and useful moral theory could hold purely on the grounds set out in (1) alone that there was more than one P-type action which was a moral absolute. It is a logical truth that not more than one moral consideration can be morally more important than all the others. (Perhaps it might be argued that this must be qualified to take account of the possibility that several P-type actions might be equally important, while all being more important than any of the remaining P-type actions. But a theory of this kind, while consistently holding that there was more than one moral absolute as defined in (1), would fail to tell us how we should act in a situation involving more than one such duty in which there was no way we could behave which would count as meeting all our obligations. Since such a theory would be useless, this possibility has been discounted in my formulation of condition (1).) On the basis of condition (1), then, there could at most be one absolute obligation or prohibition.

Condition (2) presents rather more difficulty. On the basis of this condition, there could in theory be indefinitely many obligations and prohibitions each of which was absolute, provided only that the world were such that opposing absolute obligations could never be encountered in the same particular situation. But is the world like this? Well, the evidence which we possess strongly suggests that it is not. Our experience presents us with very many instances in which we are faced with opposite and competing moral claims on us, between which we have to decide. Moreover, nothing in our experience suggests that our more important obligations are ones which are more free from such conflict than our less important ones are. At the least, I think we can conclude that we have no means of showing that condition (2) is satisfied; and, more strongly, I believe that all our moral experience strongly suggests that it is not.

My conclusion is that there is at most one moral obligation which is absolute, despite the fact that there are very many actions which are intrinsically right or intrinsically wrong. However, although this is the theoretical position, I think that it is also true that in practice we take some P-type actions to be more important than others, and we regard at least a few of them as so important that, for most practical purposes, they can be treated as if they were absolutes. Suppose, for instance, that someone were to hold that there was an absolute duty never to kill, and that there was an absolute duty to be faithful to one's marriage vows. His theoretical position would, I think be untenable for the reasons I have just given. On the other hand, his views would lead to practically insoluble problems only in situations where the only way in which he could remain faithful to his marriage vows was by killing someone. Obviously enough, the ordinary person in his everyday life is not commonly faced with such situations; indeed, it would require considerable imagination even to construct a situation in which this was the choice with which a person was faced. (A fairly close, but still not exact, parallel to this is the reported case of a woman in a concentration camp who chose to commit adultery with the commandant as part of an agreement whereby he would refrain from killing many of her fellow prisoners.) In practice, then, I think it might be possible to maintain that more than one P-type action involved an absolute duty without the theoretical inconsistency of this position ever actually leading to insoluble problems.

Even at the practical level, however, this conclusion must be treated with considerable caution. The evidence which must be adduced in order to establish the relative importance of P-type actions is just the same kind of evidence as is relevant to establishing that they involve any obligation in the first place. That is to say, we have to consider the satisfaction of justice and of rational human needs. Now, we have already seen that there is a good deal of flexibility in the theory of rational needs, in that people faced with incompossible desires can resolve the conflict in a variety of ways – preferring to satisfy one to the exclusion of another, or modifying both, and so on. Any given human life exemplifies a number of such options, and it is extremely difficult in advance to say which need ought to have been preferred to which other. For example, a person may decide not to marry because she feels that it would be better for her to continue to work as a doctor in the slums of Calcutta; yet the opposite decision might be equally defensible. To be sure, some such options would appear to most of us to be bizarre in the extreme — say, to forego marriage in order to devote all one's energies to becoming world champion at tiddly-winks, or to suffer continual pain rather than buy medicines, because one prefers to spend the money on food for one's cat. Consequently, it is very difficult to say that marriage is, or is not, more important in itself than the service of others; and although it is at first sight easier to say that marriage is more important than tiddly-winks (or pushpin, one might add, for the point is not original) and personal pain more important than the cat, it is still difficult to devise an argument to show that the tiddly-wink champion or the cat-fancier has made any kind of moral *mistake*. I therefore cannot see any easy way of demonstrating that the satisfaction of some human needs is more important in itself than the satisfaction of some others. *A fortiori*, it is difficult to show that a particular rational need is so important that the corresponding duty is absolute, even in practice. Even the need to preserve one's life is not considered absolute by most people inside or outside the Christian tradition.

The most that I think can be said is that it is hard to see how a human life can be fulfilling unless each of the basic urges which go to make up human nature is *somehow* satisfied. In practice, therefore, we have a serious duty to act in such a way as to endeavour to bring this about, for ourselves and for others. However, the specific wants via which this is actually brought about can vary very widely indeed — the unmarried *need* not be sexually stunted, nor the hermit deprived of any role in society nor the physically handicapped be unhappy.

I have laid considerable stress on respect for the facts in developing any moral theory, and I am convinced that this respect leads inevitably to the conclusion that, even in practice, there are very few P-type actions which can be considered to involve absolute moral duties. In the end, the reason for this is the rich complexity of human nature, and the very great variety of ways in which human happiness can be found. It follows, too, that there are correspondingly many ways in which P-type actions may legitimately be ranked in importance. We must respect this complexity in ourselves and in others, and be sufficiently flexible and honest to recognize that different people will have to behave very differently, and will require us to behave very differently towards them, if they are to be truly fulfilled. It is just as important to be clear about this as it is to be critical about the many ways in which people can fail to find fulfilment, or can have their fulfilment impeded by others, by the pursuit of irrational wants.

The Authority of Moral Principles

The position argued for in this essay is cognitivist; the purpose of an ethical theory is to attain knowledge about ethics, and to discover which moral statements are true and which are not. Moral principles, on this view, do not simply express our attitude to life, or decisions we have taken about how we are going to live. Their primary function is to express truths about the relationship between events, states of affairs and actions on the one hand, and the satisfaction of rational needs on the other. Moral principles thus presuppose other truths about the world and the make-up of human beings in their society and as individuals.

The first thing to be said about moral principles, then, is that they have the authority of the truth, no more, and no less. Less ambitiously, we have to recognize that truth in moral matters is not so easy to attain, and is not always recognized when it is attained. For the most part, then, moral principles will have the authority of the evidence on which they are based, and of the method by which that evidence is assessed.

The second thing to be said about the authority of moral principles is that the relationship between moral truths and our lives is perhaps usually more complex than the relationship between other kinds of truths and our lives. Moral principles are experienced as challenging, demanding, upsetting and over-riding, in ways in which other kinds of truths do not normally present themselves. To this extent, it seems to me that emotivist accounts of ethical discourse have much to say that is both important and true. I would like now to consider the challenging and demanding aspect of the authoritativeness of moral principles by considering one traditional word used to describe them in which all these emotive overtones are obviously present. Moral principles have been compared to, and even described as, laws; and, as such, they have been regarded as being somehow authoritative over against the individual, and, on occasions, as representing a threat to the individual's freedom of conscience. In what way, then, can we justify comparing moral principles to laws, or describing them as laws?

Plainly, moral principles presuppose the truth of all kinds of laws — laws of physics, biology, psychology, economics, and so forth. Furthermore, in so far as moral principles themselves can be represented as part of a theoretical system, they can themselves be regarded as laws in just the same sense as the laws of physics or biology. Laws in this sense are not imperatives, but indicatives; they are hypotheses which we use in order to describe the way things are. In this respect moral principles, being indicatives, can be true or false. Commands or imperatives cannot be true or false. One can obey or refuse to obey a command to stand up; but the command to stand up is not true or false, and to refuse to obey it is not to reject it as false. On the other hand, one can argue whether it is true or false that smoking causes lung-cancer. But one cannot properly be said to obey this law as though it were some kind of command, even if it turns out to be true; nor is it proper to say that bodies obey the law of gravity in any other than a metaphorical sense of 'obey'. The reason for this is not because lungs, or bodies, are not human agents, and that they are therefore incapable of obedience; the reason is that causal laws relating smoking to lung-cancer, or gravitational attraction to mass and distance are descriptions of the way in which things behave, not commands to them how to behave. I think it is misleading in precisely the same way to speak of human beings obeying the law of gravity, and human beings obeying moral laws. Moral laws express truths about the relationship between, say, actions and the satisfaction of rational needs; to say that one ought not to smoke is not to express a command or an imperative, but to make an assertion about the connection between smoking and the damage we will suffer if we do. A moral principle about smoking no more commands us not to smoke than the law of gravity commands us not to jump out of fortieth-storey windows.

Does this not seem an excessively paradoxical assertion to make? Does it not almost perversely ignore the *force* of utterances like

'I ought not to smoke' and still more 'You ought not to smoke'? If these utterances are no more than statements of fact, how is it that they are so often felt to be commands? If churchmen say to their congregations 'You' (or, in these democratic days, 'we') 'ought to do so-and-so', why is it that they are so often accused of telling their people what to do, and interfering with individual liberty into the bargain? Emotivists are surely right that moral language, as it is used, does not have the cool neutrality enjoyed by statements of scientific fact. Although Stevenson was wrong, in my view, to say that moral utterances both express and arouse emotions (they may or may not), I believe he is quite right in saying that the conventions governing the use of moral utterances do indeed relate such utterances to attitudes which are, in part, based on emotions. To this extent, emotive force is part of the meaning that moral utterances have.

There are doubtless all kinds of sociological reasons why moral statements are felt to be commands, and authoritarian commands at that. If parents, or teachers, or churchmen, or politicians wish to ensure that a certain pattern of behaviour is adopted, and use moral language to convey this insistence, it is not in the least surprising that such language has the overtones of a command. One of the most objectional features of authoritarianism in morals is precisely that it has so completely obscured the basically fact-stating function of moral discourse, and has made it hard to maintain the position that moral statements have to be backed up by evidence, and are not commands reinforced by sanction, to be disobeyed if one can get away with it. Still, there are perfectly respectable, non-authoritarian, uses of moral statements whose function is to persuade people to act in a particular way, and this function is, I think, connected with the imperative-force which they are often felt to have.

Underlying this are, I think, other grounds for regarding moral statements as constraints on our behaviour, and therefore as analogous to laws or commands. Many moral principles (I exclude, for the moment, principles of justice) are simply and directly concerned with the relationship between human behaviour and human welfare. Each of us has the deepest interest in his own welfare and in making sure that other people do not interfere with his welfare, and this interest is, however mistakenly or misguidedly on occasions, reflected in our motivation to behave in particular ways, and to encourage or discourage the behaviour of others. In addition it may be that, at least on occasion, we have the deepest motives for promoting the welfare of others. Statements of fact which relate to these motives will inevitably be experienced as calls to action, and therefore as analogous to suggestions or even to commands. If one of the tired hikers, down from the hills after a hot day's walking, says 'There's a pub over there', it is more than likely that he will initiate a rapid move in that direction just as effectively as any drill-sergeant issuing a command to move over there at the double. The child at table who says 'The salt-cellar is empty' is quite likely to provoke the response 'Well, go to the cupboard and get some' because his mother experienced the child's remark as a command, though it was a statement of fact, and responded with a command on her own account. In both examples, the statement of fact appealed to motives. For this reason, statements of fact involving our welfare do not leave us unmoved as other statements of fact might. To believe that a moral principle is true is usually unlike believing that Jupiter has a certain number of moons. True moral principles can usually be connected with motives calling us to action; and to remind someone that a moral principle is true is to give him, or remind him that he has, motives for acting in a particular way.

Despite this analogy between moral principles and commands, there is an important difference between them. The sanctions involved in breaking a moral principle are related to that principle in a way which is different from that in which sanctions are related to the disobedience of commands. In the case of the soldier refusing to turn right on the parade-ground, the sanction is likely to be something like being confined to barracks. There is no intrinsic connection between the refusal and the punishment. In contrast, the primary sanction for breaking a moral principle is that one will be less fulfilled as a human being than one would be if one lived by it. The motives which can be appealed to in support of acting in accordance with moral principles are precisely those urges and desires which will otherwise not be satisfied. The constraints of morality come in the first instance from the internal drives of our own human nature.

It would be extremely neat if the matter could simply be left there. A major qualification has to be made. On what I take to be the reasonable assumption that the constraints of justice will on occasion require us to forego our own genuine interests in favour of the interests of others, it will not be the case that the agent himself will always suffer if he fails to live up to the principles of justice. It will, to be sure, still be the case that *someone* will suffer; and it will also be true that good reasons could be given why the agent should accept and live by the principles of justice. But, in contrast to other moral duties, it will not necessarily be the case that the agent will be able to discover in himself any motive for acting justly, if we distinguish motives from reasons. To this extent, the demands of justice may more easily be experienced as an imposition, even if he can see that it is a rationally defensible one.

The point is somewhat wider still. Even where the agent's own welfare is concerned, and especially where it is his future welfare that is concerned, the individual agent may not at the present moment have any motivation for doing what is in his overall interest, and will therefore tend to experience moral statements to the effect that he ought to provide for the future as constraints imposed upon his present behaviour against his inclinations.

In both these cases it may well be the case that, as a result of his moral upbringing, the agent has learnt to prize behaving morally, and has developed something of an emotional commitment to so doing. Both Aristotle and Aquinas laid great emphasis on the value of such training. It is possible for a man to learn to be passionately concerned for justice even at the expense of his welfare, and to learn to derive satisfaction from the knowledge that he has acted in his own long-term interests against the more immediately obvious inclinations of the moment. Where he has learnt to feel in this way, the agent can honestly answer the question 'Why be moral' by saying that he feels genuine remorse, regret, or discomfort when he is not. Still, to the extent that these motives are not present, or only weakly present, it will not be surprising if at least on occasion moral principles are experienced from the emotional point of view in much the same way as are the commands of an arbitrary external authority. But although this may be a very natural reaction, it is still a very misleading one. It is true that part of the meaning of moral statements, as the emotivists have shown, involves a relationship between facts and the emotional attitudes we have towards them; and it is true that moral principles commend courses of action to us, and that their meaning is inadequately grasped unless this is understood; nevertheless, moral principles are primarily statements of fact, not expressions of emotion, or expressions of a policy I have decided to accept. It is only *in* describing the relationship between actions and the fulfilment of rational needs that they commend courses of action to us. Moral principles are to be accepted not because I am inclined to, nor because I simply decide to accept them, but because they are, so far as I can see, true. They are to be accepted in the last analysis because of the evidence on which they rest and the acceptability of the theory of which they form a part, and not because they are enjoined by any external authority. For this reason, it is no more legitimate to regard moral principles as unwarranted intrusions on my personal autonomy than it is to regard the law of gravity in this light when I am trying for a high-jump record. Facts place constraints on rational behaviour; and resentment of this state of affairs is simply misplaced.

In the light of this discussion, we can now deal with the claim, which has unfortunately been heard all too frequently in recent Christian discussions of morality, that moral principles somehow violate the freedom of the individual conscience.

Regrettably, it is true that the way in which moral principles have been inculcated and defended *has* often been an unwarranted threat to the conscience of the individual. Moral principles have been presented as commands, and words like 'obedience', 'submission' and even 'faith' have been used in connection with them in a way which largely obscures their proper status. Even when lip-service has been paid to the fact that they are truths, not commands, they have often been presented on the basis of totally inadequate argument and manifestly incomplete research into the factual data upon which such truths must ultimately be based. Principles of sexual ethics, for example, have been expounded with hardly any reference to the complex psychological factors connected with human sexuality, as though the only evidence which was relevant for sexual morality was the physiology which men more or less share with animals. Principles of justice have been advocated with a high disregard for economic and political reality. Such presentations really do violate conscience, for conscience consists in the ability to make rational judgments based on proper evidence and coherent argument. The education of conscience, the attempt to produce the 'formed conscience' so beloved of moral theologians, positively requires the presentation of such evidence and argument, and not the dictation of conclusions. The ultimate authority of moral principles is the authority of the truth; and truth in ethics is known only through the painstaking study of the facts.

All this, however, is a matter of the way in which moral principles are presented and supported. It is a confusion so to over-react to such abuses of the conscience of individuals that one then goes on to suggest that moral principles are inherently opposed to the conscience of the individual. Moral principles stand over against the judgment of the individual in just the same way, and to the same extent, as any true statement stands over and against the judgement of the individual. That is to say, the consequence of not believing in a true moral principle is that one is simply mistaken. Of course it is true that someone is able to believe only what he is able to believe. Circumstances may make it impossible for an individual to believe what is in fact the case. This human weakness is quite general and to be found in all areas of human thought, not just in ethics. And of course it is true that a person should act in accordance with his honest and honestly formed beliefs. But to say, quite rightly, that a person ought in this sense to follow his conscience is to say nothing about what he ought to believe. To be content with saying no more than that a person ought to follow his conscience is to ignore the crucial fact that we should be concerned not simply with blameworthiness but with moral truths.

Moral principles are, or claim to be, statements about what is the case. We must decide whether or not to believe such a statement, just as we must decide between conflicting accounts of the causes of cancer, or the best way to grow tomatoes, or the best explanation of the First World War. Such decisions, whether in medicine, horticulture, history or ethics, can be well-founded, hasty, ill-informed, and quite simply mistaken. Truth, alas, is not an inseparable companion of sincerity. Authoritarian and anti-authoritarian attitudes to ethics both stem from the same fundamental mistake, that the basic issue is whether or not to obey what is ultimately a command. Ethical authoritarians and ethical anarchists richly deserve one another. Both have forgotten that more is at stake than clarity on the one hand, or sincerity on the other. What is at stake is truth.

IV

Authority in the Christian Community

The position which I have tried to develop so far rests on two main foundations. From the theological point of view, it rests on the more Catholic and rationalist stress on the need for a natural theology and a natural law theory of ethics, which in turn reflects a theological judgement about man's ability to co-operate with the grace of God in coming to know him and his will for us. This ability, stemming from creation, is logically prior to man's acceptance of God's revelation of himself in Christ. From a philosophical point of view, I have argued that only a cognitivist position in ethics can do full justice to our ordinary moral discourse, and that only some version of a naturalist position can account for the way in which we distinguish moral from non-moral issues. Taken together, these two strands of argument lead to the conclusion that the ultimate authority in ethics is the authority of the facts in so far as these can be discovered and interpreted by the normal methods, scientific and informal, of human inquiry. I have accordingly argued that the appeal to Christian tradition cannot be an ultimate appeal; and that the appeal to moral principles as though they were ultimately authoritative misrepresents their true philosophical status.

Both on rational and theological grounds, however, the matter cannot be allowed simply to rest there. Not every appeal to an authority is based on the assumption that that authority is somehow ultimate; and the appeal to authorities has a proper and necessary place in the pursuit of knowledge. On theological grounds, the Christian must cash in practical terms his belief that the Holy Spirit guides the teaching of the Church in morals as in faith; and on rational grounds, a great deal can be said about the ways in which it is in practice essential to appeal to authorities. Accordingly, this chapter will attempt to take a more positive look at the role which authorities ought to play in the Christian community in the realm of ethics. And in particular, I shall try to say something about the Catholic belief in the infallibility of the Church in moral matters.

The Legitimate Appeal to Authority

I suggest that in human inquiry generally, it is legitimate to appeal to authorities in support of a position just in certain conditions:

(1) The question must be one which we have not settled satisfactorily ourselves.

(2) There must be some external grounds for believing that the authority appealed to is likely to be correct on the point in question.

(3) The grounds for believing in the authority must be sufficiently strong that they outweigh any tendency we may have to disagree with its conclusions on internal grounds.

(4) It is undesirable to rely on authority in circumstances where it is practicable to settle the point in question without making any appeal to authority.

There are many considerations which can be urged in favour of these conditions. That we should accept (1) follows, I think, from the very meaning of appeal to authority. If I have worked something out myself satisfactorily, then it will no doubt be true that I will agree with what authorities on the point would also say. It may even be that my confidence in my own result will be increased by the knowledge that it agrees with the conclusions of recognized authorities. But I cannot logically believe a conclusion on authority if I have also recognized that it is justified on the basis of argument. The appeal to authority is possible, then, only when there is some recognized limitation in my own knowledge.

Condition (2) is rather more obvious. There is no point in appealing to someone as an authority if there is no reason to believe that he is likely to be right on the point in question. The point is obvious enough, but can perhaps be amplified. To begin with, in order that I legitimately appeal to someone as an authority, it is not required that I believe that he could not possibly be mistaken on the point in question. All I need believe is that he is more likely to be right about it than I am; and it is desirable that I also believe him to be more likely to be right than any other authority to which I might have appealed. Moreover, the grounds for believing that he is likely to be right must be external to the evidence for the question about which the appeal to authority is being made. For if the authority convinces me by his arguments, I will believe that his conclusion is true on the basis of the arguments, not because of the status of the authority. External grounds for believing in the authority can be of several different kinds. Suppose, for example, that I look up a history of philosophy in order to discover the views of Biel, about whom I know nothing. I might be impressed by the standing of the author of the article on Biel in the scholarly community; I might also know that, in those areas of philosophy with which I am acquainted, his views are balanced and sound; the footnotes to the article on Biel might in general terms suggest that he has done a good deal of research; his presentation might be free from any readily identifiable bias, and might be conducted in a style that suggests competence, care, and so on. On such grounds, I might well accept him as an authority on Biel, although *ex hypothesi* I am unable to pass any judgement of my own on what he actually *says* about Biel.

Sometimes the situation is not quite so simple, and condition (3) is designed to take this into account. I might, for example, already have a general belief that Biel was a thoroughgoing nominalist: this is how he is frequently described in works that I have read, and some of his disciples have pronounced nominalist tendencies. Suppose, now, that my authority takes the line that it is largely mistaken to regard Biel as a nominalist, and that this interpretation rests on a misunderstanding of the meaning of some of Biel's key technical terms. In this case, I do not come to the authority with a totally unformed mind, and, as a result, I will be more or less surprised to find him taking a line so different from what I thought I knew on the subject. At this point, I have to weigh the standing of my authority against the firmness and extent of my own prior beliefs about Biel. The more I know already, the better the evidence will have to be if I am to believe that the authority is reliable in taking such a different line.

Condition (4) is of rather a different character. It deals not with the factors determining whether an appeal to an authority is intellectually defensible, but with the conditions under which such an appeal is morally desirable. It seems to me to be in accord with human dignity, and to show a proper respect for human intelligence, that we should refuse to allow ourselves to appeal to authorities in matters where we could perfectly well reach a satisfactory understanding of the question for ourselves. Thus, to take one application of this principle, we are in general perfectly content that children should rely on the authority of their parents on all sorts of matters which they cannot be expected to work out for themselves; we also expect them gradually to grow out of this dependence and stand on their own feet, as a part of their normal development. Or again, a first year philosophy student may produce perfectly acceptable work if he manages to restate clearly and in his own words more or less the conclusions of the philosophers he has read. To do even so much is often quite an achievement. But his teachers would normally expect him over the course of his studies to make progress in developing an independent judgement. Of course, practical considerations play their part here. We might have legitimate grounds for appealing to authority if the cost of learning from our own mistakes is likely to be unreasonably high, or if the effort to work things out for ourselves would take an unreasonably and unproductively long time to do. No scientist is going to insist on performing all the previous experiments on which his own research relies even if he could quite well do so. It is perfectly proper for him to take at least some of them for granted, and to go on from there.

We may now consider the relevance of these conditions in the particular case of the appeal to the authority of Christian tradition in morals.

There are many occasions on which we have little enough reason to be confident of our own moral judgement. The elaboration of the criteria for evaluating wants already given in Chapter II should have made it clear that it is often a far from easy process even to discover which of our wants express rational needs, let alone to discover the best way of choosing when incompossible wants are involved. The theory of justice is notoriously difficult. And the result is that our moral conclusions will be to a greater or lesser extent tentative. All this would be true even if we were at all times ideal moral agents, acting to the limit of our human capacities. Of course we are not always like this; we are on occasions stupid, prejudiced, too emotionally involved in an issue to be able to consider it with a dispassionate philosophical eye. To the extent that we recognize all this, we will recognize that in principle there will be occasions on which at least the first condition for the proper appeal to authority is certainly fulfilled in our case.

The Christian believes that he has general theological grounds for his confidence in the inspiration of Scripture, and the continuing guidance of Christ's Spirit in the Church. In making this assertion, he must, of course, beware of taking 'Church' in too narrow a sense; and he must, more broadly, have satisfactorily resolved the problems mentioned in Chapter I about whether there is any reason to suppose that revelation has to do with ethics at all. Leaving those issues aside, however, I shall assume in what follows that in the Bible and in the later tradition of the Church we can expect to find the guidance of the Spirit operative in matters of morals as well as in matters of doctrine. On the other hand, and leaving issues connected with infallibility aside for the moment, we are also aware of the limitations of the Church as a human community. We do not as a human community respond perfectly to the promptings of the Spirit, nor do we take all possible means to solve our ethical dilemmas with the grace of God. It follows that, issues of infallibility apart, we cannot expect the authority of the Church in morals to be absolute; and we will have more reason to believe that it is authoritative on some issues than on others.

The upshot of these considerations is that the third condition emerges as of central importance in practice. The ultimate authority in ethics is to be found in the facts about ourselves and our world on which morality rests, as these are organized in an acceptable ethical theory. Of these facts and the arguments involved we all normally have some, but not total, knowledge; and we normally have a whole series of beliefs which we would be willing to defend in varying degrees. We do not approach the moral teachings of Scripture and later Christian tradition with totally unformed minds on the subject. Our situation is parallel to my consulting an authority on Biel when I already have some idea about what a correct interpretation of Biel's philosophical views might comprise. Similarly, there are some occasions on which we can expect the moral teachings of the Church to confirm and elaborate the beliefs we already held, and this would tend to confirm our confidence in the truth of those beliefs. On other occasions, we will find that our previous moral opinions are challenged by Christian teaching. Examples of this challenge are not far to seek: men have found the pacifism of the Sermon on the Mount an outright challenge to the comparative complacency with which we are apt to assume that it is right to use violence in self-defence or in a just war; the Christian tradition on the indissolubility of marriage comes as a challenge to the *mores* of contemporary Western society; much of the prophetic tradition in Scripture and the lives of some of the great saints constantly challenge our view that there is little we ought to be doing to relieve the plight of the poor and the underprivileged. The Holy Spirit, in short, is apt to appear in the form of a Judge quite as much as in that of a Comforter. About this general situation there is no room for surprise, and every reason for gratitude. Nevertheless, careful consideration must be given to how we should respond in each individual case.

What was said about exegetical and hermeneutical problems in the first chapter makes it clear that the mere fact that we find the authority of Christian tradition challenging does not of itself enable us to say precisely how that challenge is to be responded to. We need to have some tolerable assurance that it is indeed the Spirit that we are listening to through the all-too-human voices of tradition. So it is that some Christians have considered themselves bound by the Gospel to be pacifists, while others, equally conscientious, have not. Christians differ in their views on divorce, not because they are unaware of the texts of their tradition, but because they are divided on the extent to which those texts have been fully understood and properly applied. So far as ethics is concerned, it is my view that the relationship between the authority of tradition and our own moral conclusions is a dialectical one. In any particular case, the proper response will depend both on our clarity about what has been said in tradition and the reasons for which it was said, on the one hand, and, on the other, the confidence which we can properly place in our own moral beliefs formulated independently of that tradition.

We may take the two sets of claims separately. To begin with, we must ask how certain we are of the meaning of the texts to which we might appeal; we must also ask how much we understand about the circumstances in which their teaching was formulated, and about the reasons for which it was held to be appropriate. On occasions, too, it will be relevant to ask how carefully a particular moral inquiry was pursued, what evidence was considered important, and to what extent it reflected the prayerful consensus of the whole Christian community. Positive results to these inquiries will lend weight to the view that in that tradition we are likely to discover the authoritative voice of God. All this evidence must then be taken in conjunction with our grounds for confidence in our own moral beliefs. Is the subject one which is within our experience? How broad is our experience at this point? How emotionally balanced are we on the point in question, and how intellectually honest in our arguments? Are there cogent grounds for saying that morally relevant circumstances exist which differentiate our situation from that in which previous traditional teaching was formulated? Plainly, the balance between the two sides of the equation will vary considerably from issue to issue. To take two extreme examples. We might have every reason to believe that we have given a balanced, thorough and well-informed account of a moral problem, without perhaps being totally confident about our own conclusions — say, that slavery was wrong in the eighteenth century in the Americas, and may even have been unjust in the circumstances of the Roman Empire. Against that, we might hold that the long-standing Christian tradition allowing slavery was clearly conditioned by historical and cultural considerations, and based originally on somewhat inadequate scriptural support. At the other extreme, we might have an issue on which we have little confidence in our own objectivity — say, the extent to which a Christian should renounce material wealth — and where Christian tradition throughout its history and in many different cultures has spoken with one voice. In such a case, it seems to me that it is likely that the teaching of tradition could be appealed to with some confidence that it conveyed the guidance of the Spirit, despite our own hesitations to embark upon a course of action which runs counter to so many of our current moral assumptions about what counts as deprivation.

So far as the fourth condition is concerned, it is clear that the Christian should mistrust the tendency to widen the range of topics in which appeal is made to authority, simply on the general grounds that one would in general terms suppose that more was known about human nature and the effects of our actions on human welfare than was known previously; the sciences of medicine, biology, psychology, sociology and economics have not stood still, after all; and, besides, there ought to be a general assumption that the appeal to authority should be progressively less necessary, rather than progressively more necessary, if we are to have a proper respect for individual responsibility.

The proper Christian response to the tradition of moral teaching and belief in the Christian community is therefore neither one of unquestioning acceptance of everything which has been said, nor an iconoclastic refusal to recognize that authority in morals has a legitimate and, on occasion, an essential role to play. It is simply not the case that once man has 'come of age' he no longer ever has any need to appeal to authority, whether in ethics or in anything else. Rather it is that, once he has come of age, he is better able to judge when he stands in need of authorities, and to estimate the value of various authorities to which he might appeal on a given subject. In such a case, it seems to me simply mistaken to present individual conscience and authority as somehow inherently opposed to one another. Precisely conscience itself, our balanced and informed moral judgement, will on occasion demand that authorities be consulted and followed.

Infallibility in Morals[1]

No account has so far been taken of the Catholic belief that there are, or can be, instances in which the authority of tradition is to be taken as absolute. Surprisingly enough, there has been comparatively little discussion of the particular issues raised by the belief that the Church can teach infallibly about morals, and few attempts to analyse just what can be expected of the Church when it does teach in this way. There are perhaps several reasons for this. Since it is hard, and perhaps even impossible, to find any examples of such teaching being given by papal definition in morals, and since other possible instances of such teaching may be somewhat harder to identify with confidence, it may have appeared that the subject was of comparatively little practical importance. Perhaps, too, there has been some confusion between the well-founded assertion that for the Christian tradition must be authoritative, and the less well-founded assertion that it follows that this authority must in practice be treated as if it were absolute, even if infallibility is not in question. Perhaps, too, it has been too easily assumed that the issues which could be raised about infallibility in morals are no different from those involved in the belief about infallibility in matters of doctrine. Nevertheless, it seems to me that the difference in subject matter between morals and doctrine has important implications for the practical import of the doctrine of infallibility, and for the kind of authority which such teaching in morals could be expected to have.

The strategy of my discussion of infallibility in morals runs as follows. I shall attempt to say what the word 'infallible' means. I shall then try to avoid what I have taken to be sources of some confusion, by giving an account of the difference between necessary and timeless truths, and the relationship between these notions and the notion of irreformability which was linked with infallibility by Vatican I. I shall then ask in what sense, if at all, one could expect infallible teaching in morals to be timeless, irreformable, and unchanging, and what the practical implications of such teaching might be.

---

[1] I have modified, but not radically altered, my position in the light of Tierney's helpful reply to my earlier article.

'Infallible' and 'irreformable'

The First Vatican Council predicated infallibility of the Church and of the Pope, in certain circumstances, and irreformability of certain of their teachings. I believe that this distinction is a valuable one to maintain, in that it helps to avoid some confusions which might more easily arise were we to speak of 'infallible teachings' or 'infallible truths'. In particular, to speak of 'infallible truths' might suggest that some special *type* of truth might be involved in such cases, and that 'infallible truths' are true in a different way from that in which non-infallible truths are true. I think it is somewhat more likely that this impression might be given by the use of 'infallible' than by its more precise partner 'irreformable'. I would however be willing to accept the current common usage in which not merely persons (Pope or Church) but also teachings or truths may be spoken of as infallible, provided that the precise longhand equivalent is kept firmly in mind. Infallible truths are those truths taught by an infallible teacher.

What is meant by 'infallible'? Consider the following two statements:

(1) If an infallible person asserts that something is true, then it necessarily follows that it is true.

(2) If an infallible person asserts that something is true, then what he asserts is a necessary truth.

The first of these statements might be used as a definition of 'infallible' and is itself a true statement precisely because of what the word 'infallible' means. Thus, if an infallible tipster asserts that Long John Silver will win the Derby, it necessarily follows that Long John Silver *will* win the Derby. Were some other horse to win, our tipster would not have been infallible after all. Of course, we may not have any grounds for believing that there *is* an infallible tipster; but that is another question. Statement (1) states what would have to be true of such a tipster if there were one. In the same way, we must separate the theological grounds on which we might justify the belief in an infallible moral teacher from what such a belief means. Catholics believe, on theological grounds, that in certain circumstances the Church can teach infallibly about morals, and that this teaching can be expressed through the Pope.

The meaning of that belief is that, when such teaching is propounded, it necessarily follows that that teaching is true.

Statement (1), following as it does from the meaning of the term 'infallible', is true, and is not at all the same as statement (2). Statement (2) is about the *kind* of truths which infallible teachers can teach, and asserts that they teach necessary truths. Statement (2) is contrary to Catholic belief, for it is part of Catholic belief, I would argue, that the Church has infallibly taught that the Son of God became incarnate in the Middle East in the first century; but plainly, he need not have done so at that time, or in that place, or even (most theologians would hold) at all. That he did so is therefore not a necessary truth. It is no part of Catholic belief in infallibility that infallible teaching consists of necessary truths.

Is it part of Catholic belief that infallible teaching must consist of timeless truths? A case could be made for saying that all necessary truths are also timeless truths, and it is easy to see how someone who mistakenly believed that infallible teaching had to be about necessary truths might also conclude that it therefore had to do with timeless truths. He might then go on to equate the notions of 'infallible truth', 'necessary truth', 'timeless truth', and use these notions to explain the crucial concept of 'irreformable truth'. I have already shown that the notion of necessary truth is an irrelevancy so far as the belief in infallibility is concerned. The notion of a timeless truth is more complex.

One might at this point profitably introduce a distinction between sentences, statements, and propositions, but in the interests of simplicity of presentation I shall try to avoid these technicalities without, I hope, falsifying the position too much. Consider (i) injustice is wrong; (ii) there are three persons in God; (iii) Britain is a member of the Common Market.

The first of these might be taken to be true by definition; it is a necessary truth, and in one fairly clear sense is also a timeless truth. It is not as if injustice is wrong at one time and not at another; at any given time, injustice is wrong. In contrast with this, (ii) is neither tautologous nor true by definition; and, although Christians believe that it is a necessary truth, the sense of 'necessary' here is different from that in which 'Injustice is wrong' is a necessary truth. Somewhat similarly, (ii) is a timeless truth, not because it is true at any given time, but because it is concerned with a reality which is not time-bound at all. Nevertheless, both (i) and (ii) will be true whenever they are asserted, albeit for somewhat different reasons, and to that extent might both reasonably be described as timeless truths. In contrast, (iii) does not appear to be a timeless truth at all. After all, there certainly was a time when there was a Common Market of which Britain was not a member; and it could conceivably be the case that there will be a time in the future at which Britain will have ceased to be a member. Still, it is also the case that since Britain in 1978 is a member, it will remain true that Britain was a member in 1978; and it has always been true that Britain would be a member in 1978. Similarly, it is true for all time that Caesar crossed the Rubicon, although it could not be said that he is crossing the Rubicon now. To put the matter in other words: the 'is' in 'Injustice is wrong' and in 'There are three persons in God' is tenseless, whereas the 'is' in 'Britain is a member of the Common Market' is tensed; yet, despite this fact, there is a sense in which, if something is ever true, it timelessly-is true, in that what was true can never turn out to have been false. We must make a careful distinction between the tenseless way in which timeless truths like (i) and (ii) are to be understood, and the way in which even tensed statements like (iii) can still be said timelessly-to-be true. All truths timelessly-are true, but some are tensed, and some others are not tensed.

Now, we have already seen that it necessarily follows that what an infallible person teaches is true. It follows also that such a teaching timelessly-is true, in the sense that it can never turn out that such a teaching was, after all, false. On the other hand, it does *not* follow that infallible teachings must themselves be tenseless rather than tensed. In the light of this, I propose the following account of the meaning of 'irreformable': what is taught infallibly is irreformable precisely in the sense in which *any* truth is irreformable; it can never turn out to have been false. If it is true that Caesar crossed the Rubicon, it timelessly-is true that he did, and it will never in the future turn out to be the case that he did not; and if it is true that John will go to America next year, it will never turn out to be the case that he didn't after all. This is simply part of what is meant by 'true'; it is of the nature of truths. Vatican I did not say that the Pope was infallible of himself and independently of the consent of the Church; it said that infallible teachings were irreformable of themselves, and not because the Church decided to accept them. This doctrine seems to be very accurately put. If some teaching was true, then whether or not anybody continues to believe it it can never turn out to have been false; of its nature, a truth is irreformable.

It would be most unfortunate, however, if belief in the irreformability of infallible teachings were to give rise to the belief that they must necessarily be tenseless. Some infallible teachings are tenseless — such as that there are three persons in God; others are not, such as that Christ died for our sins. Just as the irreformability of the truth that Caesar crossed the Rubicon does not entail that he is crossing it now, neither does the irreformability of the teaching that Christ died on the cross entail that he is still dying there now. And the fact that there tenselessly are three persons in God is a consequence not of the fact that this is infallibly taught, but of the reality with which that teaching is concerned.

At this point, then, we may distinguish between irreformability and the need to reformulate the ways in which we give expression to the truths we believe. Plainly, we frequently require to reformulate irreformable truths; for example, we wish to translate them into a different language; or to express them in other words within the same language. Plainly, too, there are many difficulties involved in being sure about whether a proffered reformulation is adequate, or whether it does not rather alter what was being said. Thus, to take a recent example, people might disagree about whether the Agreed Statement on the Eucharist is no more than a reformulation of the truths in which they previously believed, or whether those truths have been altered in the process. Into these (very serious) problems I cannot enter here. For my present purposes it is enough to underline that there is one reformulation which is absolutely obligatory if we are to continue to express the same truth. 'I am sitting at my typewriter' expresses a truth at the moment of writing, and the 'am' is tensed. To express that same truth tomorrow, I shall have to say 'I *was* sitting at my typewriter'; and, tomorrow, it may or may not express the truth if I then also say 'I am sitting at my typewriter'. The sentence 'I am not sitting at my typewriter now', uttered tomorrow, does not at all call in question that the sentence 'I am sitting at my typewriter' uttered now expresses a truth, despite the fact that the sentences might *appear* to be logically contradictory.

Timelessness in morals

I have argued so far that the belief that the Church does, or could, teach infallibly about morals leaves open the further question about the logical status of the moral truths which are infallibly taught. Further, the belief that these truths are irreformable in themselves and not because of the agreement they command is simply the belief that, because of the nature of truth, what is true can never turn out to be false. We may now consider in the light of the doctrine of infallibility the various kinds of moral truths already examined (above, pp.72–83). In that discussion, I distinguished three types of action, three ways of describing behaviour, which might turn up in moral principles. In the same way, I shall now consider some examples of these three types of principle, and how they relate to views about timelessness and irreformability.

A   Murder is wrong

P   Giving pleasure to someone is right
     People should be given a balanced diet

F   Building a large house is wrong
     Having sex before marriage is wrong

What distinguishes the first two types of statement from the third can be discovered by an examination of the subject-terms in each case. We have already seen that the ultimate justification for the ascription of any moral predicate must have something to do with human welfare or harm. In the case of both A-type and P-type actions, that relationship between action and welfare or harm is part of the meaning of the words themselves; murder by definition involves harming a human being; giving pleasure to someone by definition contributes to their welfare, as does giving someone a balanced diet. On the other hand, building a large house is not, by definition, either helpful or harmful to people, although it may in fact harm or help in any particular case. Still, just the meaning of the words does not, without further information, enable us to tell whether it helps or harms. Similarly, it may be that sex before marriage in fact harms people; it may be that (as many would believe) it does not; but the meaning of the words in which the action is described does not of itself tell us which.

What distinguishes the first case from each of the other two is that the very meaning of the term 'murder' guarantees that when a piece of behaviour is once correctly identified as murder, there are no further moral considerations which need to be taken into account before giving a final moral assessment of that behaviour. This is not the case either with P-type or with F-type actions, obviously.

I think it is fairly clear that both A-type principles and P-type principles are tenseless truths (when they are true at all). It is not the case that murder is wrong now, but could conceivably be right at some future date; nor is it the case that giving someone pleasure, other things being equal, could be right today and wrong tomorrow. In the case of A-type principles, they are tenseless by definition: and in the case of P-type principles, we can at least say that, since these principles simply reflect the nature of human beings as they are, these principles are tenseless in the same sense in which statements about human nature are. In my view, it is not conceptually possible to conceive of a time when human beings, other things being equal, will no longer require a balanced diet; evidence that a person no longer required such a diet would be evidence, in my view, that that person was no longer human.

It follows from this that neither A-type nor P-type principles need to be reformulated in terms of their tenses in order to retain their truth value. They are in this respect not like 'Caesar crossed the Rubicon' or 'Christ died on the cross'. Moreover, since there are very many moral truths of type-P, and, no doubt, several of type-A, there is no reason in principle why the Church should not infallibly teach them. Furthermore, there is no reason why the Church should not teach that any A-type principle expresses a moral absolute; such principles do so by definition. On the other hand, I hope to have shown that at most one P-type principle can be taught as an absolute principle, since it simply cannot be true that there is more than one; infallibility presupposes truth.

The situation with F-type principles is more complex. F-type actions as such are not intrinsically connected with either harm or well-being. On the other hand, they may either in a particular instance, or in very many, or even in all such instances, in fact bring about such harm. Whether they do so or not is a matter of evidence, and cannot be decided just by examining the type of action in itself. Thus, we may be in a position to say that, in the vast majority of cases, building a house contributes to human welfare, and even (though perhaps with less confidence) that building a large house does so. But if we say this, we do so on the basis of evidence about the type of shelter which people need, and the effort they will have to expend in keeping up large houses, and the employment which such construction projects provide, and so on. On the other hand, evidence seems to be mounting that building large 40-storey blocks does not contribute to human welfare, or will do so only if several other conditions are carefully met. Similarly, it may well be that to have sex before marriage harms people; but whether it does so or not is a matter of evidence, and will depend on all kinds of factors, psychological, sociological, legal, and so on. The same can be said of other F-type actions, such as paying someone £100 per week. Whether or not this harms the person will depend on all kinds of economic and indeed personal factors.

Now, once a particular F-type principle has been established as true, there is absolutely no reason why it could not be infallibly taught. And if it is true, it will be irreformable; it can never turn out to have been false. However, it is quite another question to ask whether F-type principles can be tenselessly true in the way in which P-type and A-type principles are. Each case must be examined on its merits, and there is no general answer possible. For example, take the F-type action 'making someone swallow cyanide' (which must be carefully distinguished from the P-type action 'giving someone an unbalanced diet'). One might perfectly understand the meaning of 'cyanide' and not know whether swallowing cyanide harms human beings or not, or in what quantities it harms them. The description of the action in itself tells us nothing. The situation might be (as I believe it is) that, because of the laws of our physiological make-up, swallowing even small quantities of cyanide is always extremely harmful, and usually fatal. Once again, this is a matter of evidence; but I take it that the evidence in this case is such that it is highly doubtful whether we could conceive of a human being of whom this evidence would not hold. If so, the F-type principle 'Giving people cyanide to swallow is wrong' would be tenseless. In contrast to this, we might consider the principle 'Lending money at interest is wrong'. Whether or not this practice is harmful or beneficial will depend on a wide variety of circumstances. It may well be that in a particular economic climate or within a particular economic system it is harmful, and not in another. It may also as a matter of fact be the case that these circumstances vary with time. In such a case, it may well have been true in 1550 that this practice was wrong, and false in 1978 that this practice is wrong. The F-principle is therefore not tenseless.

The appeal to infallibility in morals

The appeal to authority is possible and desirable precisely in those cases where the person is aware of inadequacies in his own knowledge. It is, of course, possible that a person might be ignorant even of A-type or P-type moral principles, or might be unsure of them, either because of his youth, or his limited intellectual capacities; and it is therefore possible that he might have to appeal to authority even about these principles. However, the more difficult and the more interesting problems arise not with A-type or P-type principles, but with F-type principles, and it is on these that I shall concentrate.

If the appeal to infallible teaching in Christian tradition is to be made at all, it is essential that instances of such teaching can be identified, and that we should be perfectly clear about precisely what is being taught. This difficulty applies both to faith and to morals. Thus, it may not always be clear whether something is being taught *ubique, semper, ab omnibus,* nor whether, if it satisfies that condition, it is being taught as an essential part of Christian belief. And even in those cases in which it might be clear that some infallible teaching is involved, it may still not be clear precisely what that teaching is (any more than the belief in the inerrancy of the teaching of Scripture solves all the problems of discovering precisely what that teaching is). In this respect, I think that there is no difference between the problems in discovering infallible teaching on matters of faith and those of discovering infallible teaching in matters of morals.

But the two areas of infallibility differ in important respects. Most importantly, infallible teaching on matters of faith must normally at least concern matters which are in the strictest sense revealed, and about which we have no independent way of finding out for ourselves. There is therefore an inherent problem in distinguishing between our difficulty in understanding the meaning of the text, and our difficulty in comprehending the ways of God. We cannot, in short, use our independent knowledge of what is true in order to discover what it is that the text must mean to anything like the extent we might otherwise like to. To be sure, we can use our knowledge of cosmogony or history to prove that certain beliefs about what the Bible teaches must be false, and cannot be part of God's revelation. But in matters of faith, the use of this technique is strictly limited. On the other hand, I hope to have shown that we do have independent ways of discovering what is true in ethics. To this extent, it is always in principle possible for us to use this knowledge in trying to assess whether something has been taught infallibly in the tradition. Since we know that anything taught infallibly must be true, we can at once say that anything we can independently discover to be false cannot possibly have been infallibly taught. In principle, this technique will be applicable to any moral truth; and in practice, will be applicable to a greater or lesser extent according to the degree to which our moral beliefs are well founded.

The second way in which differences between faith and morals is relevant is this. Many of the truths of faith are tenseless truths — for example, the dogmas of Trinitarian doctrine, the doctrine of creation, and much of the doctrine of grace. Many others, although they are tensed, are now all to be expressed in the past tense — for example that Christ died on the cross for our sins, or that he rose for our justification, or that God became man in Jesus. There will be no further need for reformulation of these doctrines in respect of their tense. But many of the most interesting moral principles are not tenseless, for many true F-principles are tensed, and further reformulations in respect of tense cannot be excluded. Thus, whereas we might be prepared to say that if it was infallibly taught, in the fifth century, that Jesus was both God and man, we can still say that he is both God and man. We cannot conclude that if some F-principle (say, that usury was wrong) was taught in the late middle ages, we can still say that usury is wrong.

In the case of F-principles, then, the appeal to infallible authority is likely to be a rather complex proceeding. Suppose, for example, that the overwhelming consensus of Christian tradition in the middle ages was that there could be instances of justified war; and suppose that someone today was unsure whether in 1978 there could be such an instance, and wished to appeal to the teaching of tradition to settle his doubt. He has, we will suppose, some grounds for believing that no war in modern conditions could be a just war. Firstly, he will have to ask whether the medieval consensus satisfied the conditions for an infallible teaching, a question to which no convinced contemporary pacifist could give an affirmative answer, and to which our questioner might himself be in doubt about the correct answer to give. Then, even if he satisfies himself that the medieval teaching was infallible, he still has to discover whether the F-type principle 'Some wars can be justified' is tensed or tenseless. This second question cannot be settled simply on the grounds that the F-type principle was infallibly taught. Whether or not an F-type principle is tenseless is a matter of evidence, and it is just this evidence about which the enquirer was uncertain in the first place. It seems to me that so far as F-type principles are concerned, the doctrine of infallibility is of no *additional* practical importance over and above the more general considerations in support of the legitimacy of the appeal to authority which is not infallible.

In practice, however, the main emphasis of Christian moral teaching has fallen on P-type principles rather than F-type principles, and it seems to me that this tradition is so overwhelming and constant that it has good claims to be considered as infallible in many cases. I have in mind the constant teaching of such P-type principles as respect for human life, the legitimacy of private property, the importance of care for the needy, the duty of forgiveness and the wrongness of revenge. To this tradition someone who doubted the truth of any of these principles could appeal with the greatest confidence, and perhaps even with total confidence.

My general conclusion then must be this. There are occasions on which it is legitimate, and indeed may be one's duty to appeal to authority in endeavouring to settle one's moral dilemmas; and the Christian will in the first instance look to the moral teaching of Christian tradition in order to discover the authorities to whom he can turn. To a somewhat greater extent than in matters of faith, he will always be weighing up the authoritativeness of any particular teaching of the tradition against the evidence he has for his own beliefs. For the most part, and especially in the case of F-type principles, the doctrine of infallibility in morals will make little practical difference to this general picture, because the identification of such infallible teaching in the end rests on just the evidence already in question. The authority of Christian tradition is a great help to us in our moral dilemmas; our belief that that tradition can be infallible does not provide automatic solutions to them.

Pluralism

It will readily be seen that an approach to ethics such as I am proposing will lead to a much greater variety of moral opinion than a more authoritarian approach would. Indeed, it is a consequence of my view that we are likely to find people arriving at different estimates of the meaning and import of the authoritative tradition itself, even when they do appeal to it for guidance. And I have already noted that some theologians have been concerned that any natural law approach to morality will inevitably lead to a completely shapeless and uncertain Christian ethic. It might even be alleged that such is the diversity of human moral opinion that the attempt to base ethics on any account of human nature will end up in relativism. I wish first to set out as clearly as I can the kind of pluralism to which, as it seems to me, I am committed, and to show that it is desirable rather than undesirable that there should be such pluralism in ethics. Then, in the final section of this chapter, I wish to rebut the charge that anything I have said could lead to relativism.

That there should be a certain pluralism in the views we may defensibly hold about ethics is an inevitable consequence of the inadequate evidence on the basis of which we must form our moral beliefs. It is, for example, inevitable that there should be a wide diversity of opinion about what we ought to do to help the poor of the Third World, simply because our knowledge of economics, sociology, and what one might call political psychology is so inadequate, not to speak of the shortcomings of our present technology. I take it that there *is*, ideally, some answer to the question 'What ought I to do to help the poor of the Third World?' which is both specific and correct. But I have no idea what that answer might be. Again, to the extent that our knowledge increases, pluralism resulting from ignorance will tend to disappear. It may have been a point for discussion thirty years ago whether a doctor ought to give pregnant mothers thalidomide; at least now we know that he should not. It may have been arguable that high-rise flats ought to have been built to rehouse the urban slum-dwellers; we now know that the solution cannot be so simple. We now know that it is immoral to treat certain mental illnesses as instances of demonic possession. Some of the moral controversies of the past can be resolved, just because we have more and better information at our disposal.

That there should be this pluralism is unavoidable in any ethical theory which is based on the end on factual information. It is from an ideal standpoint undesirable that we should be ignorant of the facts on which moral decisions depend, and this kind of pluralism is not to be upheld as somehow valuable in itself. On the other hand, the moral to be drawn is that we should make every available effort to dispel our ignorance. It would be fundamentally mistaken to attempt to reduce this kind of pluralism to unity by the authoritarian imposition of views which go beyond the evidence and experience available.

Very different, and in my opinion thoroughly desirable, is the ethical pluralism which springs from the recognition of the almost inexhaustible variety of human nature and the rich diversity of the many ways in which human beings can find fulfilment. Even within a given culture there are very many different vocations and careers and sub-cultures in which diverse patterns of life and fulfilment develop. The way of life of a crofter in Skye, a motor-worker in

Coventry, and a university lecturer in Hampstead are quite different from one another, and involve very diverse patterns of value-preferences and duties. Even though it is true that the same set of basic human urges is being catered for in each case, the emphasis put on each of them is very different, as is the set of wants in terms of which each of these individuals learns to interpret his needs. None of these individuals would find it altogether easy, and might even find it almost impossible, to adapt to the life of one of the others once he has happily settled into his own.

The point is even stronger when we consider what we would informally term different cultures. Cultures with a strong stress on the value of the individual and his liberties will exhibit quite a different pattern of rights and duties in their moral behaviour from cultures where the emphasis is on the extended family and the value of communal relationships. To be sure, there are common constraints on all these patterns of life which have to be observed if a particular culture is to succeed in promoting the well-being of its members. Those to do with physical welfare are most obvious: there must be food, and shelter and health-treatment, and these goods must be provided systematically for the weak as well as for the strong. More inter-personal constraints are more difficult to identify. But in any culture there must, if people are to be happy, be a pattern of relationships which supports and provides stability for the individual, education for the children, and within which each person can find a role in his society. Nevertheless, the particular ways in which these very general needs are met can vary enormously. Certainly, it is the case that people have believed that these needs were catered for in very different ways; we have polygamous and monogamous societies, individualist and collectivist ones, democratic, oligarchic and monarchic ones. Societies feel the need of different levels of technological development, different sexual *mores*, different views about property, the care of the aged, the legitimacy of killing, and the relationships between parent and children, husband and wife and so on. I am not saying that all these cultural variations must be accepted without criticism; on the contrary, most of this essay has been devoted to outlining the avenues along which such criticism ought to proceed. Still, even when all my four criteria for discovering which of our desires

represent rational needs have been correctly and completely applied,
I see no reason to suppose that the result would be to show that
all men ought to have precisely the same wants. I would regard
any theory of ethics as disastrously wrong if it had the consequence
of requiring that there should be some grey undifferentiated manner
of life in which we all had to engage. It seems to me that there
could in principle be indefinitely many sets of wants which differed
from one another, and yet were all expressions of equally rational
needs. In each set, the various elements would be nicely balanced
one against another, representing various options between defensible but incompossible desires. This balance can be extremely
delicate. There is enough evidence from the colonial era of the
appalling results of attempting to alter one element in a cultural
pattern and expecting the others to survive undamaged. Nearer
home, we can see the difficulties of immigrant communities and the
strains produced when they attempt to adapt their traditional cultures to the British way of life. The requirement that rational needs
form a compossible set is not one which can be lightly violated.

All this is obvious enough. But it is worth asking *exactly* what it
has to do with pluralism in ethics. Does the happy crofter have a
different moral code from the happy motor-worker, the contented
Muslim peasant, and the Catholic priest? I think there is some
temptation to say that the moral code which makes a person truly
happy must be the same as the moral code which makes another
person truly happy. This approach could be defended; but I think
it is perhaps less misleading simply to say that there can be several
different and equally satisfactory moral codes. However, there is a
matter of terminology involved here, and the attempt to clear it
up may make this apparently radical conclusion easier to accept.

How is one to count moral codes? Does the unmarried priest
have to observe a different moral code from the father of a family?
Is the moral code of the Skye crofter different from that of the
Coventry motor-worker? Well, certainly each of these four people
has a very different way of life, and it is their duty to perform
very different actions. The crofter does not have to clock in, nor
the motor-worker have to consider how his use of the land will
affect his children's future. The priest has a duty to keep up his
theology, the married man to care for a particular woman. Children

in Skye perhaps should be brought up very differently from children in Hampstead or Coventry. Yet perhaps we still feel like saying that each of these people observes the same code in his own particular circumstances, and that that code is different from the one observed by nomad Bedouins, or primitive New Guinea tribesmen. This position is natural enough; but it is very questionable whether there is any theoretical basis for the distinction so sharply drawn between on the one hand a moral code and its applications, and, on the other, several different moral codes.

Assume that the four Britons, the Bedouin, and the primitive New Guinea tribesman are all contented. It could be argued that they must observe the same moral code, since they have all succeeded in developing ways of life which satisfy the same basic human urges. The differences between them represent different climactic and economic circumstances in which each of them lives. Moreover, one might imagine the principles of a moral code expressed in the following form:

Every M ought to do A

or, equivalently,

If one is an M, one ought to do A.

Values for 'M' here might include 'crofter', 'priest', 'Bedouin', 'union member in Britain' and so on. Each of the principles formed by substituting a value for 'M' and a corresponding value for 'A' will be true of all human beings if it is true of any. Thus, it is true of me now that if I am a married man I ought to care for my wife, and that if I am a member of the Imperial Guard I have certain duties towards the Emperor. One might then imagine a single (albeit immensely long!) moral code simply by conjoining all the principles held by each of the individuals I have mentioned, and claim that each of them lives by this code as it applies to him.

On different grounds altogether one might claim that there must be a plurality of moral codes. For example, one might say that there must be a different moral code for each value of 'M', consisting of just those As which Ms have a duty to perform or avoid. This set will be different, to a greater or lesser extent, from the set of As to be performed by some other class of Ms. This proposal, although comparatively clear, has the somewhat surprising consequence that not merely do Britons have a different moral code from Bedouins, but also that motor-workers have a different one from crofters, and perhaps, husbands have a different one from wives or children.

If such a plurality of moral codes seems something of an *embarras de richesses,* hardly more acceptable than the artificial unicity of the single moral code for all men, one might try to find some middle way by saying that there are as many codes as there are cultures; but the dividing lines between cultures are themselves somewhat arbitrarily drawn. I shall have something more to say about the plurality of moral codes when I come to discuss the issues raised by relativism. For the moment, luckily, it does not much matter how we count codes — the problem of the one and the many is for once more verbal than real. The real issue underlying the discussion of whether pluralism in ethics is or is not desirable comes at a different point.

The real issue is this. For how many different values of 'M' will it be justifiable to say that they should perform different As from those to be performed by members of some other class of Ms? Does it follow that if a priest should behave differently from a crofter, because he is unmarried and the crofter is not, so, too, the Bedouin with three wives should behave differently from them both? Precisely which circumstances must make a difference, and which should not? That is the nub of the problem. I have already given the only criterion I can see for settling this question. One must consider how the various actions open to that person would actually affect his fulfilment and that of the people among whom he lives, and whom he affects by his action. And the answer to this will in turn depend on the rational needs which these people have learnt to develop on the basis of the fundamental human urges which motivate us all.

The relationship between ethical pluralism and the authority of the Christian church has been, and should continue to be, a complex one. Christian tradition has developed through the gradual resolution of tensions between existing Christian communities and the other cultures with whom they came into contact and to whom they preached the Gospel. Care must be taken to avoid any identification of Christianity with any particular cultural setting and the moral patterns appropriate to that setting. Just as we should be aware of the difficulties of treating the teachings of earlier tradition as though they were all tenseless, so we must be aware of the dangers of transferring our own moral code into an alien culture as though the circumstances of that culture could make no moral difference. In each case, there is evidence to be considered before we can be sure whether we are being uncritically accepting or blinded by our own cultural prejudices. This evidence is to be sought in the actual effect that a way of life has on the people who try to live it. Acceptable pluralism is defined and justified by its fruits; and the fruits of morality are happiness and justice.

Relativism[2]

That a position is relativist is a charge more often made than made clearly; and relativists themselves have often been among the most confused advocates of their own position. It is perhaps worth clearing out of the way some inadequate formulations of relativism before trying to defend my own views against the charge that they might have relativist implications.

Perhaps the most commonly expressed view of relativism is that it consists in the theory that any individual has a duty to obey the moral code of the culture to which he belongs. This view, which Williams has described as the 'anthropologists' heresy'[3] has in more modern times been put in an even more broadly tolerant form, to the effect that each person has a duty to do what he believes to be right. Two things must be said about these positions. The first is that, just as they stand, neither *need* be a mistaken view. The first might well be correct, were it also to be the case that the person's culture subscribed to a defensible moral code. And the second might either be taken in the same sense, in which case it, too, will depend on whether the individual's beliefs are defensible; or else it might be no more than a restatement of the view that a person is obliged to do as he honestly believes his duty requires. Neither of these positions even *looks* relativist unless it is assumed that there

---

[2]   See Phillips and Mounce, and Winch, chapters 2 − 4.
[3]   Williams, p.34.

is no means whereby cultural or individual beliefs can be criticized. Secondly, even taken in the strong subjectivist sense, it would appear that these views intend to say that a person has a duty (whether to follow his cultural code or his individual opinions) in an absolutist sense of 'duty'. It really, from a neutral point of view (so to say), *is* his duty to behave in the ways specified. At this point the allegedly relativist position becomes incoherent.

The reason that these positions have often been thought to be relativist is, however, instructive. It seems to me that it has seemed relativist to say that people ought to behave differently in different cultures because it has been assumed that an absolutist morality cannot allow for so much variation as this view would apparently sanction. For just this reason, the pluralist position for which I have been arguing might well appear relativist. Part of the reply to this view is to point out, as I have above, that it is partly a matter of terminology whether one says that these cultures have one moral code applied differently in each of them, or different moral codes. An alternative way of making the same point would be to say that it certainly cannot be relativist to assert that circumstances alter cases. No moral theory worthy of consideration could possibly deny *that*. The question then is whether living in a different culture is likely to involve being placed in circumstances which are relevantly different, or whether it does not. To someone who believes that comparatively few circumstances should make any moral difference, a theory which holds that many circumstances make a difference is apt to appear relativist. The dispute is properly not about relativism at all, but about the proper criteria for deciding which considerations are morally relevant. I have tried to argue for a clear method of settling this dispute. My solution may well be mistaken; but it cannot be said to be relativist.

The distinctively absolutist feature of the views I have been proposing is precisely that culturally-neutral criteria are available in terms of which a moral position can be constructed. In some fashion or other, the true relativist has to deny this. Roughly he will have to maintain the moral behaviour in different cultures is non-comparable.

Someone who wishes, as I do, to defend an absolutist position against this form of relativism has a fairly formidable case to rebut.

It can take either the form that moral views are constituted by the culturally-relative patterns of thought in which each of us finds himself, and from the confines of which we are both logically and psychologically unable to step; or it can take the form of saying that the meaning of any action can be grasped only within the culture in which it is performed, and the attempt to compare an action in an alien culture with an action in one's own about which one already has moral views is simply to misunderstand the whole position. Thus if I, who believe that polygamy in Wimbledon is wrong, were to assume that polygamy in West Africa were the same action, and therefore must equally be wrong, I would simply have betrayed my misunderstanding of what that behaviour *meant* within the context of that culture, misled by a superficial behavioural similarity. The mistake would be only slightly less naïve than if a primitive tribesman, who had just learnt that if a motorcyclist extends his left hand he is signifying his intention of turning left, were to suppose that the traffic-policeman himself intended to turn left because he extended his left hand in the middle of a crossing.

Learning to interpret the policeman's action, however, is a fairly simple matter of learning the conventions under which policemen in Britain control traffic. Learning the meaning of polygamy in West Africa is not like this. I think that the question to which the relativist must answer 'no' and the absolutist 'yes' may be formulated as follows: is there any way in which the *moral* significance of an action in one culture can be expressed in terms of the morality of another? Only if this question can be affirmatively answered will it then be possible to go on to discuss whether that action is right or wrong in any absolutist sense of those terms. If the question cannot be answered, then there simply is no standpoint from which such an absolutist judgement can be given.

Let us take a comparatively simple example. I shall assume that the committed punk rock fan belongs to a different culture from myself, at least to a considerable degree. Suppose I now wonder what action in my life corresponds morally to his going to a punk rock concert. We would be well advised not to give too hasty an answer to this question. The most obvious answer would be 'my going to a punk rock concert too', since on the face of it I would then be performing precisely the same action as he is. But plainly this action would not occupy at all the same place in my life as it does in his. He looks forward to going, enjoys it enormously, is, indeed, almost a different person while he is there; whereas I go somewhat apprehensively, feel totally out of place, don't enjoy it at all, and return vaguely depressed and out of sorts. A slightly better answer might be 'my going to hear a string quartet at the Festival Hall', since at least here I do look forward to it, enjoy it while I am there, return refreshed. I read books about Beethoven's late quartets, just as he reads magazines about punk rock. Yet, though this answer is an improvement, I think there are good grounds for not resting content with it. For I am still vaguely aware that Beethoven doesn't mean as much to me as punk rock does to him, and there is something very different about the *way* in which he enjoys himself at his concerts and the way I enjoy myself at the Festival Hall. Precisely the morally relevant features of the two actions seem to be notably different even here.

At this point, I am forced to speculate, for I do not pretend to understand punk rock culture. What is the attraction? Is it sexual; or escape from the drabness of routine? Is it perhaps a more generalized pleasure in a kind of physical exhilaration? An over-powering sense of at last belonging? An aggressive desire to outrage conventional sensibilities? For all I know, it could be any one of these or, more probably perhaps, a blend of several elements in which one or other predominated. One thing is certain, however: I cannot even begin to identify a morally equivalent action in my life until I know what his action means to him. On the basis of my speculative musings so far, I might hazard several guesses about what I would have to do in order to do 'the same' as him. Embark on some sexual escapade? Have a week-end break touring cathedral cities? Sail a dinghy in a brisk wind? Have a few close friends round for a quiet evening? Celebrate the Eucharist? Tell everyone just what I think of them at the next committee meeting?

These guesses are highly speculative, partly because I do not understand his action, and partly, too, because I may not be alto-gether clear what *I* would be doing in each of these cases. What would these actions mean to me? It is my view that the necessary and sufficient conditions of my being able to identify in my life an action which is morally equivalent to him going to a punk rock concert are three:

(1) I must know the basic needs which my actions satisfy in me;
(2) I must know the basic needs which his action satisfies in him;
(3) I must be able to find an action of mine which satisfies precisely the same needs as those which are satisfied by his going to the concert.

Plainly, meeting conditions (1) and (2) demands a very considerable degree both of self-knowledge and of empathy and understanding of the punk-rock fan. Plainly, too, it will be impossible even to begin to satisfy (2) unless it is in principle possible to satisfy (3) as well. Unless at some level (and it may be a very basic level indeed) his needs are the same as mine, actions which satisfy his needs will appear simply unintelligible to me. On the other hand, I think there are good reasons to suppose that (3) is, in principle, satisfiable. Firstly, I think it is a conceptual truth that other human beings have the same basic urges as I have. Secondly, more empirically, experience suggests that we are able, at least to some extent, to understand people from different cultures, and for this understanding to develop and grow.

Nevertheless, the relativist who doubts whether this can be done is not wholly mistaken, although I think he is ultimately mistaken. For in the case of a culture very different from our own, direct comparison between behaviour in that culture and behaviour in our own is almost certain to be quite misleading; their learnt wants are so different from ours that their actions will be, at least on the surface and perhaps for some way below the surface, morally baffling to us. The relativist is quite correct to insist on this fact, and to insist that we do not naïvely assume that we can identify patterns of behaviour in that culture which correspond morally to similar patterns in our own. Where I believe he is mistaken is in his view that there is no ultimate basis of comparison.

If I am right so far in what I have said, then the conditions for making moral judgements of actions in cultures other than our own can also be stated. It seems to me that these conditions are the three already listed, plus a fourth:

(4) If the action in my culture is right (or wrong) then that action in the other culture which corresponds to it will also be right (or wrong) in that culture.

I would contend that the procedures outlined in Chapters II and III above outline the path along which we can in principle discover whether these four conditions are satisfied in any given case. It is also my belief that full assurance on these points will not be easy to attain. And I suspect that some condition(s) will need to be added to deal with inter-cultural comparisons involving justice.

The discussion of relativism and pluralism may appear to have taken us very far indeed from the subject of this chapter, authority in the Christian community. I do not think that this is the case. I have argued that there is a need for the appeal to the authority of tradition in ethics, and that the Christian will look, in the first place, to the traditional moral teachings of Christianity. He will do so on theological grounds. I have also been concerned to argue that the appeal to the authority of tradition, even when it is legitimate, must be very carefully conducted. The discussion of infallibility has highlighted what has been implicit in the discussion of tradition in Chapter I, that there is an essential distinction to be drawn between tensed and tenseless moral truths within that tradition; and the discussion of pluralism and relativism has stressed what was also implicit in that chapter, that inter-cultural comparisons are much more difficult to make than might appear. At least it cannot be assumed that polygamy in West Africa simply is morally equivalent to marrying several wives in Wimbledon, and appeals to authoritative condemnations of polygamy must not be carried on without examining this assumption carefully. The procedures of Chapters II and III suggest a way in which this examination might be carried out, or at least begun. That these procedures exist is the reason why the views I have advanced are not relativist. That they are difficult to carry out stems from the rich variety of human nature. It is my final conclusion that taking the concept of human nature seriously, as I have tried to do, leads inevitably to an ethical theory which is neither relativist nor monolithic. It seems to me that only such a theory can be integrated with any appeal to an authoritative tradition in a religion which has to be preached to all men.

V

Morality in the Christian Community

This essay has been concerned with method in Christian ethics, and, in particular, with the place which the appeal to various authorities ought to have in moral argument. As such, it has not been directly aimed at arguing for specific conclusions about individual moral issues, but rather with advocating that these issues should be approached in a particular way rather than in other possible ways. Now, any method will stand or fall on one or other of three counts: the coherence and clarity of the arguments offered; the extent to which a serious application of the method leads to conclusions which either run counter to or confirm our deeper and more reflective moral convictions; and the extent to which the daily practice of the moral life in the Christian community is seen to be helped by the community's adoption of the method. On the first count, all I can say is that the arguments I have presented must be judged on their merits, both philosophical and theological. Then, so far as concerns the conclusions which this method will lead to, I would say only that in my opinion these conclusions will be neither startlingly radical nor reassuringly conservative. I would expect the main lines of Christian tradition to be confirmed by the method I have outlined, and would also expect some of our more detailed answers to highly specific problems to be challenged in the light of modern knowledge. That, I think, is as it should be. To substantiate this claim would require, as I have argued, detailed examination of the facts involved in specific moral controversies, an enterprise for which I have neither the space nor the expertise. The time is surely past when moral theologians or philosophers can be regarded as able to pronounce on the most diverse issues in medicine, economics, psychology, law and politics independently of the collaboration of experts in each of these fields. The most they can do, as I have tried to do, is to indicate to the experts which are the questions which must be answered, and to demonstrate how the answers to those questions bear on what ought to be done.

Some elaboration of the third point will, however, be a fitting way of concluding this essay. The proof of the pudding is in the eating, and it is my conviction that, were the Christian community to agree on some method such as I have outlined, many of the difficulties with which it is currently plagued would to a large extent be resolved. In particular, I think that the misuse of various authorities in moral argument has led to a stifling of moral progress, and, simultaneously, to a discrediting of those authorities themselves. The result has been that Christian morality has all too often been characterized by a disastrous combination of insecurity, authoritarianism, and loss of nerve on the part of many whose task is to teach morality in the Christian community. One of the most important ways in which any approach to ethics can commend itself is by enabling us to circumvent such problems, and I would like to conclude with some reflections on how I think this might come about.

Open Moral Debate

The method I have advocated rests on two very basic general claims. The first is that there is a significant parallel between an acceptable moral theory and an acceptable scientific theory. The second is that there is no specifically Christian authority in ethics by appeal to which we can effectively hope to foreclose any moral argument: in practice, there is a most important place for such appeals, whether to the Bible, or later tradition, or to moral principles which have stood the test of time; but in theory each of these authorities owes its status as an authority to the success with which it interprets the facts, and it is to these alone that any ultimate appeal can be made. It follows from these two claims that Christian ethics will flourish best in the climate and by the means which contribute best to the flourishing of any other science. Specifically, it will flourish best when the method and approach are a matter of open argument and debate, and when the necessary factual research is thoroughly carried out and taken fully into account.

That there is widespread disagreement on the proper method to be followed in Christian ethics is evident. At all levels, from the correspondence columns of the popular press to the pronouncements of moral theologians, the divergence of approach is every bit as striking as the variety of conclusions propounded. It is assumed, often without any argument at all, that issues can be settled by quoting Scripture, or by referring to documents of the Magisterium of the Church, or by describing the difficult situation in which an individual finds himself, or by appealing to 'the natural law', political necessity, or personal guidance from the Holy Spirit. Not that there has not been much good work done. There are excellent studies of New Testament ethics, the hermeneutical problem, and the nature of inspiration, by exegetes and theologians. Moral philosophy abounds with discussions of the concept of human nature and its relationship to ethics, and with detailed considerations of particular types of moral argument. But all this seems to have made strikingly little difference to a great deal of moral theology. It seems to me that theologians, and moral theologians in particular, have all too often supposed that there is a specifically theological method, leading to a specifically theological ethics, which justified them in paying little heed to moral philosophy, or, indeed, to the philosophical problems underlying theology itself. And it is certainly true that much modern moral philosophy is conducted in ignorance of the classical debates on ethics in Christian moral tradition. I have tried to argue that theologians who either ignore moral philosophy, or who attempt to decide on theological grounds between 'good' and 'bad' moral philosophy are simply bad *theologians;* and that philosophers simply must, in their endeavours, keep in constant touch with the tradition of moral thinking, or they will be bad moral philosophers. At any rate, it seems to me quite incontestable that these issues of method should be thoroughly thrashed out in open public debate, rather than tacitly assumed without argument in the course of controversy on specific moral issues. No science can flourish in default of an agreed paradigm in which one can tell which research is relevant, and when particular conclusions have been proved or disproved; and if such a paradigm is not to hand, as at present it is not in Christian ethics, then debate must focus on that, rather than dissipate its efforts on inconclusive arguments on particular problems.

The second consequence of adopting the method I propose would be that a much greater emphasis would be laid on the basic information which is required for moral theology even to get started at all. The Christian community must at all costs avoid giving the impression that moral answers to particular problems are quite evident in advance of any research into the economic, psychological, medical, or social facts of the matter.

In part, this is a question of scientific research. Christians who adopted the method I propose would actively support research into the causes of marital breakdown, or the effects of interdenominational education in different social and political circumstances. They would wish to know much more about sexual psychology, the effects of legislating on public moral attitudes and behaviour, the actual effects of giving aid to countries, groups or individuals. In default of clear information on this level, specific moral conclusions would be proposed only tentatively and with a proper degree of caution. In my opinion, the status of Christian moral theology would be immeasurably enhanced in the world at large did it show clearly that it was anxious to share in such research and would take its results seriously, instead of giving the impression that such research is irrelevant or even positively threatening to sound morality. That kind of dogmatic insularity engenders contempt, and has, I submit, seriously damaged the credibility of the Christian message as a whole. To the extent that Christians find truth threatening, others will find Christianity disreputable.

The method for which I have argued has its implications on a more informal, and even personal, level, as well as on the level of scientific and intellectual research. The moral thinking of individuals, and the way in which morality would be taught, would reflect a genuine willingness to look at what is actually happening

in oneself and in others. Moral education would primarily be concerned with making sure that this ability to know oneself and to
project oneself into the moral world of others is as highly developed
as it can be, given the limitations we all have as individuals. Moral
principles, from wherever they may be derived, will not be an
acceptable substitute for the serious effort to improve one's moral
knowledge. Take, for example, the case of a young mother who is
wondering whether or not she ought to go out to work. If she has
been taught that moral thinking takes the form of appeal to moral
principles, she might well try to solve her dilemma by simply
rehearsing the principles she has been taught: 'Mothers have a duty
not to neglect their children'; 'A woman has a right to personal
fulfilment in a career'; 'A mother's place is in the home'; 'One
ought to provide a decent standard of living for one's family'.
Some of these principles may be true, others either oversimplified,
question-begging or false. In any event, it is surely evident enough
that the equipment they provide is quite inadequate for solving
her problem. What she needs above all is knowledge of the basic
pre-moral facts. She needs to know precisely how her actions might
affect the well-being of her husband, her children, and herself. And
in order to know that, she needs to have real understanding and
imagination to enable her to focus on the real needs, and not simply
the alleged wants, of all the people concerned.

The advantages of a proper moral method can be illustrated
from almost the opposite point of view, in the case of someone
who has over-reacted against any systematic approach to ethics at
all. Thus, someone who claims that the only significant moral
demand is that one be loving is likely, in my opinion, to pay insufficient attention to what is actually being done to themselves and to
those around them as a result of their actions. Morality on this view
can too easily become a matter of mood or intention, and respect
for the facts of the case will suffer accordingly. A well-meaning
sentimentality is no proper substitute for genuine moral imagination and what Iris Murdoch has called 'selfless respect for reality'.

On both these levels, then, the scientific and the informal, it
seems to me that nothing but good can come of the adoption of
the method for which I have been arguing. Moreover, far from this
method leading to greater uncertainty and insecurity in the Chris-

tian community, it is my conviction that the opposite effect would result.

It is certainly true that the present climate in Christian morality is heady to the point of being disorienting, and that the openness of current ethical debate is often a source of considerable insecurity. The reasons for this, are, I suggest, complex. Perhaps in some cases the insecurity is caused by mistaken beliefs, such as that one's eternal salvation depends on one having correct answers to all one's moral problems, a belief which certain presentations of Christian ethics have tended to reinforce. More generally, I think that current debate is experienced as unsettling precisely because there are no agreed rules by which it is to be conducted. In default of a defensible method, there is simply no way of knowing when questions are properly put, which are good arguments and which are not, when progress is being made and when it is not. Arguing without method is like running desperately in a moorland fog, and it is no wonder that the effect is to induce feelings of helplessness and insecurity. If real efforts were made to arrive at an agreed method which was philosophically and theologically defensible, there would be landmarks by which progress in ethics could be measured, and it would then be much easier for us all to be patient with ourselves. It is not too hard to say that we should not expect something as complex as the moral life to be totally clear to us, provided that we can see at least the general direction in which clarity might be sought. The attempt to cope with insecurity by the authoritative dictation of solutions is at best the result of an over-simple diagnosis of the problem, and at worst is quite mistaken in principle. Authority itself has no status unless there is an agreed framework within which its status can be assessed and defended. It is fundamentally misguided and seriously counter-productive to try to use authority to impose method, when the decay of authority is primarily due to the lack of agreed method on which authority itself ultimately depends.

The insecurity generated by open moral debate is also the result of another, quite different, complex of attitudes. A clue to this is to be found in the fact that the insecurity is apt to be highly selective, and confined to a few specific issues. This is in turn connected with the fact that many people, in thinking about morality, have in mind only a very restricted range of problems which they have been taught to regard as *moral* problems. Thus, people do not normally feel insecure and disoriented in face of the difficulties involved in choosing a marriage partner, or when different views are publicly canvassed about the policy to be adopted in the next Budget. Here, they are quite accustomed to having to act when the evidence is incomplete, and quite happy that alternative views should be equally forcefully advocated. The peculiar *moral* insecurity simply does not arise, because these are not normally thought of as *moral* problems. Yet, as I think I have shown, each of these is quite clearly a moral problem. What this shows is that it is not unclarity or plurality of views which is of itself experienced as unsettling, but rather the impact of regarding a problem as moral. It seems to me that at this point a problem becomes invested with all the unsettling features involved in the appeal to authority, and it is *this* which produces insecurity and upset. The tragedy of moral thinking (and in this it contrasts sharply with other areas of human knowledge) is that authorities are perceived as threats, and debate on issues on which moral authorities (whether principles, or texts, or people) can be quoted is felt to be dangerous. In short, the moral insecurity of the Christian community is the product of mistaken ways of appealing to authorities in morals, and will be removed only when the true relevance of these authorities is commonly understood.

If this common understanding is gained, it will then be possible to point out that people *already* think about a host of genuinely moral issues in the right way when they consider whom to marry, or where to live, or what job to take, or how to treat aged parents or handicapped children. There has been little tradition of appeal to authority on these issues, and hence no room for mistaking the nature of that appeal. I think a great step forward would be taken if one could encourage people to consider more controversial issues in precisely the same kind of way, and to use the authority of Bible, Church, moral principles, and the customs of their society as helps rather than as automatic substitutes for their moral thinking. In so far as the adoption of my proposed method would encourage this kind of development, it seems to me that it would result in less insecurity rather than in more, and would enable them to see the openness of moral debate as constructive and essential for the good estate of the Christian community, rather than as a threat to its stability.

Respect for Authorities

The last result of adopting this method to which I wish to call attention is the alteration for the better which it would produce in the attitude of the Christian community to the various authorities at its disposal.

In general terms, the method requires that ethical thinking should be based on adequate theoretical assumptions and factual research, on the experience of living the moral life, and on the collective wisdom of one's moral tradition. I have tried to show in some detail how each of these elements depends on each of the others. Experience without theory is aimless and unformed; theory without experience is vacuous; and both without tradition are likely to be impoverished and lacking in imaginative breadth. Now it is of course true that the individual Christian will, to a greater or lesser extent, exemplify each of these three elements in himself. But at the risk of over-schematization, it may be illuminating to look at sections of the Christian community as exemplifying these elements one at a time. Thus, the critical and theoretical basis of ethics is above all in the hands of moral theologians and moral philosophers; the factual research in the hands of experts in particular disciplines relevant to ethics. The experience of living the moral life is exemplified above all in the *sensus fidelium,* the moral awareness of the Christian community as a whole; and the handing on of the Christian tradition is an important part of the vocation of the Bishops and leaders of the Church. The work of each of these groups of people will go badly wrong if it is not carried on in constant interaction with the others. Academic moralists who are out of touch with the experience of Christian living in all its richness and variety will lack an essential criterion for judging the acceptability of any theory which they propose. Bishops who merely repeat what has been handed down will, by being uncritical and unimaginative, fail to meet the needs of their contemporary flock, and fail to respond adequately to Christians in different cultures from their own. Individual Christians who deny the necessity for moral theory, and who see tradition as a threat to their sacred liberty of conscience will deprive themselves of any coherent criticism on the one hand, and of the experience of other Christians in different ages and cultures, on the other. On purely methodological grounds, I think it is clear that these three groups must co-operate constantly and closely if the Church as a whole is to play its part in responding to the guidance of the Spirit offered to it. This conclusion is surely a very desirable one from the theological point of view, and I regard it as a point in favour of my arguments so far that they substantiate this conclusion on independent philosophical grounds.

Respect for the texts of Scripture and later tradition has been seriously undermined because these texts have been appealed to as though they were conclusive for solving any moral problem. It has not been difficult to discredit such exaggerated claims, and, once they have been discredited, it is all too easy to jump to the equally unwarranted conclusion that there is *no* defensible way in which appeal can be made to these texts. Moreover, the mistaken appeal to these texts has seriously falsified the nature and import of the texts themselves, in a fundamentalist direction, and has consequently encouraged a false picture, equally discreditable, of a voluntarist and ultimately arbitrary God. I have argued that the first step to be taken is that the true nature and function of these texts must be respected, so that we can see what help they can and should be allowed to give us, and what it is unreasonable to ask of them.

Much the same point can be made about the appeal to moral philosophy, and particularly the appeal to 'natural law' in more recent Catholic tradition. The philosophical arguments have often been so jejune, or slanted in advance, that it has been all too easy for theologians and for individual Christians to suppose that no real insight is to be gained from any moral philosophy at all, let alone any in the natural law tradition. Appeals to natural law have fallen on increasingly deaf ears, precisely because the full value of that philosophical tradition has been lost in the attempt to extract from it detailed solutions without the research which that tradition above all should have demanded. Small wonder that a Christian version of 'situation ethics' continues to attract when that type of view has on the whole been discredited long ago in more secular philosophical circles.

Finally, the attempt to teach moral principles has been frequently vitiated by mistaken views about their nature and the evidence on which they must ultimately be based. As a result, moral principles have come to be regarded as authoritarian intrusions on the individual conscience, and words like 'intrinsic', 'absolute' and 'objective' have become the shibboleths of an increasingly confused and acrimonious debate.

In each of these areas, it appears to me that adoption of a method such as the one I have proposed is a necessary first step for any reinstatement of authority in Christian ethics. Only in the context of such a method can authority be respected, precisely because it is no longer seen as authoritarian. In making this contribution to the debate, I do not imagine that I will have convinced everyone, or, still less, that everything I have said will turn out to be true. What I do hope is that what I have said will attract the argument and discussion which is altogether indispensable in man's search for the unchanging truth of God.

Select Bibliography

Chapter I

Barth, K., *Church Dogmatics*, II, 2 (Edinburgh, T. & T. Clark, 1957).

Brunner, E., *The Divine Imperative* (London, Lutterworth Press, 1942).

Bultmann, R., *Jesus and the Word* (London, Fontana Books, 1958).

Dorr, D.J., 'Karl Rahner's Formal Existentialist Ethics', *Irish Theological Quarterly* 36 (1969) pp. 221–29.

Fitzmeyer, J., 'The Matthaean Divorce Texts and Some New Palestinian Evidence', *Theological Studies* 37 (1976) pp.197–226.

Fuchs, J., *Human Values and Christianity* (London, Gill & Macmillan, 1970).

Gustafson, J.M.,
(1) *Can Ethics be Christian?* (Chicago, University of Chicago Press, 1975);
(2) 'The Place of Scripture in Christian Ethics: A Methodological Study', *Interpretation* 24 (1970) pp.430–55.

Hughes, G.J., 'A Christian Basis for Ethics', *The Heythrop Journal* 13 (1972) pp. 27–43.

Kierkegaard, S., *Fear and Trembling*, transl. R. Payne (Oxford, Oxford University Press, 1939).

Lindars, B.
(1) 'The Bible and Christian Ethics' in G. Dunstan (ed.), *Duty and Discernment* (London, S.C.M. Press, 1975) pp. 64–75;
(2) 'Imitation of God and Imitation of Christ', ibid., pp.100–10.

Quine, W.V.O., *Word and Object* (Cambridge [Mass.] , M.I.T. Press, 1960).

Rahner, K., *The Dynamic Element in the Church*, Pt. I (London, Burns & Oates, 1964).

Robinson, N.H.G., *The Groundwork of Christian Ethics* (London, Collins, 1971).

Sanders, J.T., *Ethics in the New Testament* (London, S.C.M. Press, 1975).
Simpson, M., 'A Christian Basis for Ethics?', *The Heythrop Journal* 15 (1974) pp. 285–97.
Ward, K., *Ethics and Christianity* (London, Geo. Allen & Unwin, 1970).

Chapter II

Clark, S.R.L., *The Moral Status of Animals* (Oxford, Oxford University Press, 1977).
Daniels, N. (ed.), *Reading Rawls* (Oxford, Blackwell, 1975).
Frankena, W.K.,
(1) 'The Naturalistic Fallacy', *Mind* 48 (1939) pp. 464–77.
(2) 'Love and Principle in Christian Ethics', in A. Plantinga (ed.), *Faith and Philosophy* (Grand Rapids [Mich.], Eerdmans, 1964) and in K. Pahel and M. Schiller (eds.) *Readings in Contemporary Ethical Theory* (Englewood Cliffs [N.J.], Prentice-Hall, 1970).
(3) 'The Concept of Morality' in Wallace and Walker (*q.v.*).
Gosling, J., *Pleasure and Desire* (Oxford, Clarendon Press, 1969).
Hare, R.M., 'Descriptivism' in his *Essays on the Moral Concepts* (London, Macmillan, 1972).
Harrison, J., *Our Knowledge of Right and Wrong* (London, Geo. Allen & Unwin, 1971).
Kant, I., *Groundwork of the Metaphysic of Morals*.
Kenny, A., *Action, Emotion and Will* (London, Routledge and Kegan Paul, 1963).
Kuhn, T.S., *The Structure of Scientific Revolutions* (Chicago, University of Chicago Press, 1962).
Macquarrie, J., *Three Issues in Ethics* (London, S.C.M. Press, 1970).
Miller, D., *Social Justice* (Oxford, Oxford University Press, 1976).
Monro, D.H., *Empiricism in Ethics* (Cambridge, Cambridge University Press, 1967).
Moore, G.E., *Principia Ethica*.
Nakhnikian, G., The Naturalistic Fallacy' in H-N. Castañeda and G. Nakhnikian (eds.), *Morality and the Language of Conduct* (Detroit, Wayne State University Press, 1963).
Rawls, J., *A Theory of Justice* (Oxford, Clarendon Press, 1972).
Stevenson, C., *Facts and Values* (New Haven, Yale University Press, 1963).
Swinburne, R.G., 'Objectivity in Morals', *Philosophy* 51 (1976) pp. 5–20.

Thomas Aquinas, *Summa Theologiae,* I-II.

Urmson, J., *The Emotive Theory of Ethics* (London, Hutchinson, 1968).

Wallace, G. and Walker, A.D.M. (eds.), *The Definition of Morality* (London, Methuen, 1970).

Chapter III

Anscombe, G.E.M.
  (1) 'Modern Moral Philosophy' in G. Wallace and A.D.M. Walker (eds.), *The Definition of Morality* (London, Methuen, 1970) pp. 211–34.
  (2) *Intention* (Oxford, Blackwell, 1958).

Casey, J., 'Actions and Consequences' in J. Casey (ed.), *Morality and Moral Reasoning* (London, Methuen, 1971) pp. 155–205.

D'Arcy, E.A., *Human Acts* (Oxford, Clarendon Press, 1963).

Goldman, A.I., *A Theory of Human Action* (Englewood Cliffs [N.J.], Prentice-Hall, 1970).

Griffin, J., 'Consequences', *Proceedings of the Aristotelian Society* 64 (1963–4) pp. 167–82.

Harris, J.,'Williams on Negative Responsibility and Integrity', *Philosophical Quarterly* 24 (1974) pp. 265–73.

Norman, R., *Reasons for Actions* (Oxford, Blackwell, 1971).

Raz, J., *Practical Reason and Norms* (London, Hutchinson, 1975).

Richards, D.A.J., *A Theory of Reasons for Action* (Oxford, Oxford University Press, 1971).

Ross, W.D., *The Right and the Good* (Oxford, Clarendon Press, 1930).

Scruton, R., 'Attitudes, Beliefs and Reasons' in J. Casey, op. cit., pp. 25–100.

Smart, J.J.C. and Williams, B., *Utilitarianism: For and Against* (Cambridge, Cambridge University Press, 1973).

Snare, F., 'The Definition of Prima Facie Duties', *Philosophical Quarterly* 24 (1974) pp. 235–44.

Chapter IV

Boatright, J.R., 'The Practicality of Moral Judgments', *Philosophical Quarterly* 23 (1973) pp. 316–34.

Goldman, H.S., 'Dated Rightness and Moral Imperfection', *Philosophical Review* 85 (1976) pp. 449–87.

Hughes, G.J., 'Infallibility in Morals', *Theological Studies* 34 (1973) pp. 415–28.

Phillips, D.Z. and Mounce, H.O., *Moral Practices* (London, Routledge and Kegan Paul, 1970).

Tierney, B., 'Infallibility in Morals: A Response', *Theological Studies* 35 (1974) pp. 505–17.

Williams, B., *Morality: An Introduction to Ethics* (Cambridge, Cambridge University Press, 1972).

Wilson, B., (ed.), *Rationality* (Oxford, Blackwell, 1970).

Winch, P., *Ethics and Action* (London, Routledge and Kegan Paul, 1972).

ㄥ